earth jems™

1

Sausage Egg cup

PASTA · PENNE · FUSILI

CONTENTS

Created and written by:
KEENA STAINBROOK

Photography by: **REETA TREAT, JESS & KEENA STAINBROOK**

Final Cover and Book Layout, Editing:
JESS STAINBROOK

Draft Cover, Book Design:
JOELLE BECKETT

FIRST EDITION

EarthJEMS™ Publishing - 1st ed.
The Essential Gluten-Free, Dairy-Free, Paleo & Vegan Friendly Cookbook by Keena Stainbrook

ISBN 9781795435338

www.earthJEMS.com

Thanks

I have so many people to thank for their support of this project. First and foremost, I am honored to serve an amazing Creator who put us together and gave us this Earth and provided everything we need to be healthy and thrive. I am so thankful for my husband, Jess, who is my biggest cheerleader and the brains behind the design and detailed editing of the cookbook! Many thanks to my girls for their very honest opinions as I created and modified many recipes to create great flavors and healthy meals. Thanks to my best friend, Monika, for all of her encouragement, recipe testing, and input into this project. Reeta Treat, thanks for your incredible photography skills and eye for making my food look tasty! Many thanks to Joelle Beckett who worked many hours to lend her design wisdom for pulling all the pieces together! I am also thankful for the support from Dr. Marie Starling and the staff at The Healing Center Denver. Thanks to all my friends, family and clients for your valuable feedback and encouragement!

> I BELIEVE THAT EVERYTHING HAS BEEN PUT ON THIS EARTH FOR US TO BE NATURALLY HEALTHY.
> –KEENA

Key

You will notice throughout my book that each recipe has this legend key next to it, so you can quickly and easily identify recipes that are designed specifically for different food sensitivities.

G Gluten-free

D Dairy-free

P Paleo Friendly

V Vegan Friendly

Restorative Diet Friendly

Writing this cookbook has been a long process. I am new to cookbook writing, for sure, but for a much bigger reason; I feel like I am continuing to grow as a natural chef. Daily I work to create a healthier version, a more tasty twist, a better understanding of how to put ingredients together. My family, friends and clients have assured me that my recipes yield delicious results and have encouraged me throughout the process. Hopefully, this pursuit will just have to yield more cookbooks filled with new, creative and fun recipes. And considering my family rarely eats the same meal twice, I am sure that will be the case!

I have no official authority to write to you as a chef, recipe developer, or cookbook author. I have not been to culinary school nor have I ever written a book. I do not have a degree in nutrition. However, I do have Mom power! And anyone who is a mom or knows a mom, knows that when a mom puts her mind to something, no one can stop her. I have poured my heart, soul, and life into improving my children's health. Since the discovery of various reactions my children were having to the food on their plates and in their bowls (the very food I cooked and thought was good for them), I have made it my mission to learn and understand what is happening to food and our health as a result. Food allergies and reactions are ever increasing. My concern is not just for those with immediate reactions. I see farther down the road as more and more people have cancers, weight issues and a low quality of life because of pain. I feel passionate about helping to educate anyone who wants to know because we need to know how to protect ourselves and heal our bodies.

As a mother, I need to protect, educate and prepare my children. So, I read and learn as much as I can. As a result, I set my mind on changing our diet. The result: Health! My kids felt great! Their skin rashes, or tummy aches, or brain fog, or weight gain all began to change. They didn't even know they didn't feel great until their diets changed. They had to adjust to eating differently than their friends but they knew how much better they felt. I slowly shared with them what I had been learning. Mission 1 accomplished. Mission 2: I had to figure out how to come up with new recipes, how to change old favorites, how to substitute to make meals and snacks that were free of gluten, dairy, egg, soy, and corn, but (and here was the challenge) were still delicious. That's key too!

These meals are meant to be quick and relatively easy. They will provide variety, something that I have learned is very important to getting all the nutrients your body needs. I wasn't much of a cook when I began this process, but in embracing a bigger goal, which was feeling amazingly healthy and improving the health of my family, I have been filled with a passion for the creativity of cooking. So I offer you this cookbook as a start on a journey toward having the tools to create healthy, tasty meals for your family.

-KEENA

THE Essential Pantry

"BE PREPARED, FOR WHEN YOU CHOOSE TO MAKE HEALTHY CHANGES IN YOUR EATING, YOUR ENTIRE LIFE WILL CHANGE FOR THE BETTER."

-KEENA

THE ESSENTIAL PANTRY

The kind of pantry you maintain at home will directly affect your attitude about cooking and shopping. Being well stocked with the right foods and having a plan each week will make it easier to stick to healthy eating and prevent stress by having to run out to the store before each meal you cook.

The Dry Goods Pantry

Herbs/Spices: Choose organic spices and herbs. Often store brand organic is the best price. Use a spice within 3 months or get rid of it. They lose their flavor and nutritional benefits after exposure to the air for that long. **TIP:** Grow your own! Find a sunny window, a cute planter and mix several herbs together in the pot. They are easy to grow and fun to just cut off a sprig and use it for dinner. With fresh herbs, I most often use cilantro, oregano, parsley, thyme, basil and rosemary. I like to have a few spice blends as well, like Italian seasoning, Tandoori seasoning, Mexican seasoning, Herbs de Provence, and Steak seasoning.

Tomatoes: Always have canned tomatoes and tomato sauces available. I prefer the brands that are organic and boast that they only use hot water to peel the tomatoes before packing. Since Italy doesn't use GMO or chemicals like US grown non-organic produce, they are a delicious and safe bet.

Beans: It is always nice to have garbanzo beans in the pantry to make hummus for a snack with veggies. Any other beans you eat occasionally like black, white or kidney beans are great to have on hand too.

Water Chestnuts: Great addition to a quick stir fry.

Bamboo Shoots: Add to a stir fry.

Hearts of Palm: Add to salads.

Banana Peppers: Salad additions.

Roasted Red Peppers: Great with pan fried chicken, salads, or steamed veggies.

Tahini: Sesame seed paste.

Juices: Lemon, lime, pomegranate.

Garlic: Fresh cloves or canned minced.

Coconut Milk: Good for adding healthy fat and creamy taste.

Jam or Jelly: Pick ones with only sugar, not corn syrup or other preservatives. Raspberry, mixed berry, orange marmalade, apricot and peach all pair well with balsamic vinegar for a quick sauce over pan cooked chicken breasts.

The Dry Goods Pantry (con't)

Oils: Use organic oils. I like to have avocado oil, canola oil, sunflower oil and grape-seed oil for high heat cooking. I use olive oil, sesame oil and walnut oil for low or medium heat.

Coconut Aminos: Also they now make a coconut amino teriyaki sauce, a gluten-free (GF) hoisin sauce, and a GF peanut sauce.

Sweet Red Chili Sauce: Adds a little sweetness and spice to any veggie or rice dish. MaePloy is my favorite brand.

Ketchup: Lots of choices here. Pick one with no corn syrup.

Fish Sauce: A great addition for a little salty flavor.

Worcestershire Sauce: Make sure it is GF.

Vinegars: Coconut vinegar, red wine vinegar, apple cider vinegar, rice vinegar.

Nutritional Yeast: This is a great addition to GF noodles in place of Parmesan cheese.

For Baking

Flours: There are more and more choices in GF flours. Here are the GF flours you should have on hand:

Arrowroot Starch: This is a substitute for corn starch in gravies, rues, sauces, etc. It is also in a lot of GF baked goods in place of tapioca, corn or potato. It is neutral in flavor, thickens well, and in my experience is the "least allergenic." This is used in very small quantities, i.e., 1 tsp-1T for thickening, ¼ C for baking in most baked goods.

Tapioca Starch: This is also a neutral thickener and starch in GF baking.

Brown Rice Flour: A good neutral choice for baking. It is higher in protein and more nutritious in baking than white rice flour. It can be too heavy to use all brown rice in a baked good.

White Rice Flour/Sweet Rice Flour: These varieties are both made with white rice. White rice flour is made from long grain white rice. Sweet Rice flour is ground up Sticky Rice. It has a higher starch/sugar content. Both work well in sweet baked goods. I like to make sure the grind is extra fine so the baked good is not grainy in texture.

Sorghum Flour: This is an easy flour to work with in GF baking.

THE ESSENTIAL PANTRY

For Baking (con't)

Oat flour: If you can eat GF oats, this flour is delicious in cookies. It gives an oaty taste to anything you put it in. I like a little in my chocolate chip cookie recipe. I just substitute out about a ½ C of rice flour for the oat flour.

Baking Powder: Choose organic and aluminum-free.

Baking Soda

Xanthan Gum: A little makes a difference in baking. Your baking products will be less crumbly. As a general rule, ½ tsp per cup of flour if you are experimenting with your own recipes.

In the Freezer

I don't use my freezer for much other than frozen meats and a few frozen veggies.

Applegate Frozen Sausages: Chicken and sage, chicken and maple, etc. They are all delicious and easy. They are pre-cooked so you can throw them in a pan and have a quick protein for breakfast on the run.

Potatoes: Sweet potato fries, waffle fries (for the Chick-Fil-A emergency cravings from a teenager in my house), hash browns. *Choose an organic variety and check for any additives or preservatives.*

Veggies: These make a great addition to rice for a quick meal. Corn, peas, carrots and shredded zucchini.

Waffles: Vans or Kashi frozen GF waffles.

Meats

Beef: Choose a grass-fed beef cut. *Corn-fed cattle are sickly because they have been fed on crowded feed lots and pumped with antibiotics so they don't get sick in the crowded, feces-laden corrals.* That's all to say on that, this is a cookbook, I don't want to ruin your appetite!

Chicken: If you can afford organic chicken, it's great. But if you need to pick somewhere to save money, here is a pretty safe place to do so. Choose chicken that is antibiotic free if you can. Hormones are banned from chicken products (at least for now!) so you don't have to worry about that.

Frozen Fish and Shrimp: Pick wild caught and not farmed fish and seafood. I love to buy the little shrimp that are precooked and add to salad or noodles.

Hijicama and carrots

BREAKFAST

> friend

"

AFTER COMMITTING TO EATING IN A HOLISTIC WAY, MY FAMILY IS HAPPY AND HEALTHY!

-KEENA

Breakfast is the meal that starts your day, and gets your body moving!

GRANOLA BARS

These are a snacking necessity. This snack packs variety, protein and nutrition not found in many snack bars. And making them yourself saves quite a bit of money when the organic bars you find in the store average $2.50 or more per bar.

2 C GF oats or GF brown rice granola
$^1/_3$ C packed brown sugar
$^1/_3$ C ground flax
1 tsp cinnamon
1 C GF flour*
* (½ C almond flour, ½ rice flour, 3T coconut flour)
¼ C raw sunflower seeds
¼ C raw pumpkin seeds
¼ C pecans
½ C cranberries, or raisins
¼ C chopped dried figs
pinch of sea salt
½ C honey
1 T chia seeds, ¼ C warm water- soak chia for 2 minutes (or use 1 egg)
$^1/_3$ C grape-seed oil
2 T vanilla extract

- Preheat oven to 350°. Grease 9x13 inch baking pan.
- In a large bowl, mix together the dry ingredients. Add the wet ingredients and mix until all is moist. Pat the mixture evenly into the prepared pan.
- Bake for 20 minutes until the bars begin to turn golden at the edges. Cool for 5 minutes, then cut into bars while still warm. Bars will stay together and be slightly chewy, not crunchy, when cool.

VEGAN PANCAKES

These are fluffy and delicious pancakes. They are egg-free and nut-free. They can be dressed up by adding banana, apple or blueberries. This makes enough for 5 people to have 4 pancakes each, however, the recipe also performs well doubled for a large breakfast crowd.

2 C coconut milk or cashew milk
1 tsp apple cider vinegar
1 C brown rice flour
¼ C arrowroot starch
2 tsp baking powder
1 tsp baking soda
½ tsp salt
¼ ground flax
1 C GF oats
¼ C dried cranberries or 1 T brown sugar

OPTIONAL ADDITIONS:
THESE PANCAKES ALSO TASTE GREAT WITH A BANANA OR CORED APPLE AND ½ TSP CINNAMON ADDED TO THE BLENDER, OR 1 C OF BLUEBERRIES STIRRED IN AT THE END.

- Put all these ingredients right into a blender and blend for 30 seconds to one minute. Allow the batter to rest for about 5-10 minutes while the griddle or pan heats up. Heat a non-stick griddle or pan to medium, spray with oil or use a bit of Earth Balance butter.
- Cook small palm-size pancakes for 2-3 minutes until they hold their shape when a spatula gently lifts their edge. Generally vegan pancakes don't bubble as much on top as traditional wheat pancake batter, but you can see that they are set and ready to flip.

earth jems

SKILLET SWEET POTATO, SAUSAGE, AND SPINACH HASH

This is a great breakfast or anytime meal. It has a sweet and a spicy component to it. You can serve it with eggs on the side if you want to use it similar to a breakfast potato dish.

2 small-medium sweet potatoes, peeled and diced (or one large)
1 apple - peeled, cored and diced
1 T coconut oil
¼ tsp cinnamon
1/8 tsp nutmeg
1 lb mild Italian chicken sausage or uncured sausage of choice, casing removed
2 to 3 C baby spinach (heaping size)
1/3 C sweet yellow onion, diced
salt and pepper to taste

- In a large nonstick skillet, heat 1 T coconut oil over medium-high heat. Once heated, add onion and diced sweet potatoes. Add a pinch or two of sea salt and cinnamon to the pan. Cook sweet potatoes until browned lightly and softening. Add apples and cook a few more minutes until apples soften, but don't cook so long that the apples loose their shape and texture.
- Remove from the pan and add to skillet the chicken (or pork) sausage making sure to break the sausage up in small pieces while it cooks. Once the chicken is no longer pink in color and completely cooked, add the sweet potato mixture back in and add spinach to the skillet. Don't worry, the spinach will wilt down when cooked. The spinach should wilt down within 1 to 2 minutes. Serve warm.

MY KIDS LOVE WHEN I POUR A LITTLE BIT OF MAPLE SYRUP OVER THEIR SERVING.

KEENA'S BANANA BREAD

3 bananas mashed
2 T chia seeds ground and added to $^2/_3$ C warm water (or use 2 eggs)
1 tsp vanilla
¼ C brown sugar
¼ C coconut oil
¾ C almond flour
¼ C arrowroot starch
1 C brown rice flour
½ tsp salt
1 tsp baking soda
1 tsp baking powder
½ tsp xanthan gum
1 tsp apple cider vinegar

- Mix bananas, chia eggs or chicken eggs, vanilla, brown sugar and coconut oil. Add in almond flour, rice flour, arrowroot starch, salt, baking powder and baking soda, xanthan gum, and apple cider vinegar. Mix until combined well. Allow to sit for 1-2 minutes.
- Place in a greased bread pan. I use a Wilton bread pan that is 8½ x 4 x 2½. Bake at 350° for 55 minutes or until toothpick comes out clean.

CARROT CAKE GLUTEN-FREE FLAX MUFFINS

These muffins are reminiscent of a carrot cake, but without all the sugar. The flax gives them great nutritious punch. Filled with veggies and fruits, these muffins make a great breakfast when paired with a smoothie or as a snack.

1½ C ground flax
½ C brown rice flour
¼ C ground chia (mix into 1 C hot water, set aside until gel forms)
1 tsp baking soda
¼ C brown sugar
¼ C honey
½ tsp salt
1 tsp cinnamon
2 carrots shredded
½ C raisins
2 apples shredded
1 C chopped walnuts
¼ C coconut oil, melted (or grape seed oil)

- Mix dry ingredients, add wet and stir until combined. Put into muffin tins (use liners or oil the muffin tins).
- Makes 16 muffins. Bake at 350° for 30 minutes.

I ADD CHOCOLATE CHIPS TO CREATE A MORE DESSERT-LIKE VERSION OF THIS RECIPE FOR MY KIDS!

BREAKFAST EGG CUPS

Invest in a set of silicone muffin cups. These egg cups release best from silicone molds. There are almost endless varieties to make. So have fun making new combinations.

Basic recipe for 12 egg cups:

> 8 eggs (choose free-range pasture raised eggs)
> ½ C unsweetened almond milk
> ½ tsp salt
> ¼ tsp pepper

Mix-ins (use any combination to your taste!):

- sausage
- spinach, red pepper, chives
- mushrooms, prosciutto ham
- bacon, artichoke hearts
- ham and onion
- make up your own!

- Mix the eggs, milk, salt and pepper until well blended. Add any combination of meats and veggies. Pour into silicone muffin cups until ⅔ full. Bake at 400° for 20 minutes. Enjoy hot and fresh or cool and refrigerate for a great protein snack later.
- TIP: For a fancy presentation, put the thin sheet of prosciutto in the bottom of the muffin mold and then pour eggs on top. Edges will stick up and be nice and crispy.

Asian Chicken Salad

SALADS & DRESSINGS

> "
> NOTHING LIKE A GREAT SOCCER GAME TO PICK YOU UP!
> –KEENA

Light and fresh, greens and salads can pick you up or lead off a meal to keep you healthy.

RANCH DRESSING

Who doesn't miss ranch dressing? Well, this recipe has delicious flavor. It is high in protein and gluten-free, egg-free, and dairy-free. Great for a party dip if you decrease the water.

1 C soaked raw cashews (2 hours)
¾ C water
2 T fresh lemon juice
½ tsp garlic powder
½ tsp onion powder
¼ tsp pepper
¼ tsp salt
1 T minced fresh basil, 1 tsp dried
1 T fresh dill weed, 1 tsp dried

- Place cashews, ¼ C water, lemon juice, garlic powder, onion powder, and salt in a blender and process until smooth and creamy. Decide if you want a thick dip or a thin dressing and add the rest of the water (up to a ½ C).
- Add the basil and dill weed and pulse briefly, just to mix. Store in a sealed glass mason jar in the refrigerator.

CASHEW CREAM DRESSING

1½ C raw cashews
¼ C water
2 tsp fresh lemon juice
2 cloves garlic
½ tsp sea salt

- Place the cashews in a bowl, add cold water, soak 2 hours.
- Combine all and blend 5 minutes. If necessary drizzle water to desired consistency.

MANGO GREENS SALAD

A fresh summer or winter salad. Mangos are available year round, but most tasty during North American winter, since it is summer in the Central and South American countries where they are grown. Use a variety of rich greens including kale and baby chard. Even add some grilled chicken to make it a complete meal. This is sure to become your favorite.

    ¼ C rice vinegar
    1½ tsp Dijon mustard
    2 T honey
    ¼ tsp salt
    pepper to taste
    ¾ C walnut oil
    3-4 C salad greens
    1 mango, diced
    ½ C dried cranberries
    5-10 mint leaves, chopped

- In a blender combine vinegar, mustard, honey, salt, pepper. Mix on medium for 30 seconds. Slowly add oil in a steady stream. Continue to blend until emulsion is complete, about 15-30 seconds.
- In a large salad bowl, combine lettuce greens, mango, cranberries and mint sprigs (chop if desired). Toss to coat.

earth jems

KOHLRABI SALAD

This salad is yummy! Most of you may never have even had a kohlrabi. The flavor reminds me of a mellow broccoli taste and crunch when raw. It can be prepared many ways, but this is my favorite crunchy salad for summer.

1 tsp caraway seeds
3 T olive oil
1 T white wine vinegar
1 T Dijon mustard
salt and pepper to taste
2 medium kohlrabi
small head of frisee lettuce
1 crisp apple
4 T fresh chives

- Use a mandolin to slice apple and kohlrabi in thin slices. I peel my apple and kohlrabi, slice in half and run on the thin setting with my mandolin.
- In a 2 C measuring cup or small bowl mix oil, vinegar, mustard, salt and pepper.
- Chop chives. Pour dressing onto the kohlrabi, apple and chive mixture and stir until coated. Serve immediately or chill first.

"

A LITTLE SUN EVERY DAY BOOSTS YOUR NATURAL VITAMIN D PRODUCTION, A KEY VITAMIN FOR SUPPORTING OVERALL HEALTH.

-KEENA

HUMMUS

Hummus is now readily available in the grocery stores and comes in a variety of flavors, but cost can be a factor. It costs less than a dollar to make your own rather than $3-5 per 6 oz tub. You can be creative with your mix-ins…roasted red pepper, green chili and cumin, avocado and cilantro.

> 1 can (15 oz) chick peas
> 1 T fresh lemon juice
> 3 T tahini
> 1 clove of garlic, minced
> 2 T olive oil
> ½ tsp salt
> ½ tsp cumin
> 2-3 T water

- Throw all the ingredients into the Vitamix or food processor and blend for 45 seconds.
- Store hummus in Tupperware in the refrigerator for up to 1 week.

G
D
P
V

HONEY DIJON VINAIGRETTE DRESSING

This honey Dijon vinaigrette recipe is delicious with a tossed green salad. However, its best feature is heated up. It makes a tangy sauce for grilled chicken.

> ¾ C extra virgin olive oil
> ¼ C white balsamic vinegar (or white wine vinegar)
> 1 T Dijon mustard
> 1 T honey
> salt and pepper to taste

- Combine the mustard and vinegar in a glass cup and whisk them together briefly. Place the mustard-vinegar mixture along with the oil, honey and seasonings in a blender and mix for about 10 seconds or until fully combined.
- Transfer back to glass container or bowl and let stand for 30 minutes so the flavors meld. Give the dressing a good whisk immediately before serving.
- Makes 1 C of dressing.

G
D
P
V

earth jems

DAIRY-FREE TZATZIKI

½ C grated cucumber
1 C cashews soaked for 2 hours
1 tsp apple cider vinegar
2 T lemon juice
¼ C water
½ tsp sea salt
1 large clove of garlic, crushed or finely diced
freshly ground pepper to taste

- After the cucumber is grated you need to squeeze the extra water out of the cucumber. This can be accomplished by placing the cucumber in a screen style strainer and just pressing firmly on the cucumber. In a blender mix the cashews, vinegar, lemon juice, water, salt, garlic and pepper.
- At the end add the cucumber and mix on low (2-3) on your Vitamix.

Refrigerate the sauce in a glass jar and it will keep for about 2 weeks.

CUCUMBER SALAD

A refreshing summer salad that pairs well with a grilled steak or juicy burger.
It has the fresh Mediterranean flavors and a salty finish.
It is equally pleasing in the winter served with Israeli Meatballs (page 77).

2 tomatoes, chopped
1 cucumber (halved, seeded, and chopped)
1 large kosher dill pickle
½ C green olives w/ pimentos
½ C black olives
¼ C parsley
¼ head shredded lettuce
¼ C olive oil
juice of 1 lemon
salt/pepper to taste

- Mix all the ingredients together and serve. It's that easy!

earth jems

BROCCOLI SALAD

This is a mayonnaise-free broccoli salad. It is just as delicious!

1 lb broccoli
¾ C slivered or chopped almonds
½ C raisins
6 slices bacon
¼ C olive oil
¼ C red wine or apple cider vinegar
salt and pepper to taste

- Preheat oven to 375°. Place the bacon slices on a baking sheet and bake until they're brown and crispy, about 10-15 minutes.
- While the bacon is cooking, get out a large bowl. For the broccoli, use your hands to remove the leaves on the base of the broccoli. Peel broccoli stems with a peeler to get to the light green center. Chop up the stem into tiny, bite-size pieces and do the same with the florets.
- In a large bowl, mix broccoli, vinegar, almonds, raisins and salt & pepper.
- Once the bacon is done, remove from the oven and let it cool. Once cooled, chop or use your hands to crumble up the bacon and add it to the bowl. Toss everything to combine.
- Serve immediately, or wait until it's cold. It's good either way.

Kale Chips, page 89

G
D
P
V

DELICATA SQUASH SALAD

1 delicata squash, or butternut squash*
3½ T olive oil
sea salt
8 cups veggies, kale, chard, spinach, radicchio-salad greens

For the dressing:
2 tsp lemon juice
1 tsp Dijon mustard
2 tsp balsamic vinegar
1 tsp lemon peel
2 T sunflower seeds
2 T pepitas (raw pumpkin seeds)

- Preheat oven to 350°, cube the squash, toss with 2 T olive oil, sprinkle with sea salt.
- Make dressing with lemon juice, mustard, vinegar, lemon peel and seeds. Once squash is cooked, cool 5 minutes and toss with salad greens and dressing.

*Delicata squash is a winter squash with distinctive longitudinal lines of dark green on a yellow background. It has a sweet orange yellow flesh. It belongs to the same family as summer squash including patty pan, zucchini and yellow squash. They grow easily, so try planting some next year in your garden.

Delicata Squash, Spinach and Pecan Salad, page 32

Chicken Pot Pie, page 71

BRISKET WITH SAGE, THYME AND MINT

This can be done in a slow cooker or in the oven.
This recipe includes directions for cooking it both ways.

1- 4 lb brisket
salt and pepper to season meat
¾ C chopped parsley
½ C chopped mint
2 T chopped thyme

2 T coconut vinegar
6 cloves of garlic
1 C chopped yellow onion
2 C beef or chicken stock

TRADITIONAL OVEN METHOD

- Preheat oven to 350°. Season the brisket with salt and pepper and place in roasting pan. Roast for 1 hour.
- In a food processor or blender, place parsley, mint, thyme, vinegar, garlic, onion, salt and pepper. Pulse until it makes a thick paste.
- Remove brisket from oven and add 2 C of beef or chicken broth slowly to pan. *I only use beef broth if I have made my own because many beef broths contain yeast and other flavor preservatives.*
- Spread the paste over the top of the meat, cover pan with foil or roasting lid and continue roasting 2-3 hours, basting about every hour.
- Remove brisket from oven & transfer to cutting board and allow to rest for 10 minutes.
- Slice against the grain and serve with pan sauce over the top.

SLOW COOKER METHOD

I use the Cuisinart Slow Cooker/Roaster. It browns, roasts, and slow cooks. So, if you don't have that kind, brown your meat in a skillet for 1 minute on each side before adding to your slow cooker.

- Trim brisket and season with salt and pepper. Heat slow cooker to "brown 350" and brown for two minutes per side. Reduce temperature to slow cook high.
- In a food processor or blender, place parsley, mint, thyme, vinegar, garlic, onion, salt and pepper. Pulse until it makes a thick paste.
- Pour the broth slowly into slow cooker and cover the meat with the paste. Cover with lid and allow to slow cook for 2-3 hours.
- Remove the brisket and allow meat to rest for 10 minutes.
- Slice meat against the grain and spoon pan sauce over the top.

earth jems

BEEF LO MEIN WITH SPAGHETTI SQUASH

This is an amazing grain-free stir fry. It is easy to make.
Note: It takes 30-40 minutes to roast the spaghetti squash.

1 lb grass-fed rib-eye steak, thinly sliced (or your can replace with browned ground beef)
3 cloves garlic, minced
1 small onion, diced
3 T GF soy sauce or coconut aminos
1 T fish sauce
1½ limes, juiced
1 tsp fresh minced ginger
1 tsp coriander
1-2 C veggies of choice-carrots, celery, cabbage
3 C fresh spinach leaves
3 green onions, sliced
1 medium spaghetti squash
olive oil
salt and pepper

- Heat your oven to 400°. Split the spaghetti squash in half lengthwise. Place split side down in a 9x13 pan. Fill with one inch of water. Roast squash for 20 minutes.
- While the squash is cooking, heat a bit of olive oil in a large pan and sear the rib-eye steak over medium high heat, about 1 minute on each side. Remove from the pan and set aside. Sauté the onion and garlic until softened. Add your veggies of choice, putting in the ones that take a longer time to cook first. Add the spinach last. Mix the coconut aminos, fish sauce, chili garlic sauce, lime juice, powdered ginger, and coriander in a glass measuring cup. Slice the steak very thinly and add to the veggies. Add the sauce and stir around to combine and then turn the heat off.
- Once the squash is cool enough to handle, fork out the threads and add them to the sauté pan. Mix everything together, stir to combine. Top with green onions and serve. Serves 6.

BISON SLIDERS ON COLLARD GREENS

1 lb ground bison
1 tsp dried oregano
1 tsp dried basil
1 tsp dried parsley
½ tsp sea salt
¼ tsp pepper
1 T olive oil

- Mix beef together with herbs and salt and pepper. Form into small patties with your hands. Heat 1 T olive or coconut oil in a skillet on medium heat. Place patties in skillet.
- Brown for 4 minutes each side (or you can grill the patties). Meanwhile, prepare collards and carrots.

COLLARD GREENS

1 bunch of collard greens
2 large carrots
1 T apple cider vinegar or water

- Remove hard stems of collards and chop into bite-size pieces. Shred the carrots.
- Place in non-stick skillet on medium heat.
- Add 1 T vinegar or water, cover, and simmer for 6 minutes until greens are tender and bright green.
- Serve greens on plate and place two mini sliders on top.

earth jems

CHICKEN MEATBALLS

Meatballs are a fun and easy protein addition to any meal. This recipe is very versatile. Add a variety of vegetables to mix it up. Just be sure to keep ratios the same. Some great veggies to try mixed in are shredded beets, kohlrabi, celery, turnips, or cauliflower.

1 lb of organic ground chicken
¼ C raw sunflower seeds
1 clove of garlic, finely chopped
2 scallions, finely chopped including green parts
¼ C finely shredded carrot
¼ C finely chopped Swiss chard or spinach
2 T chopped cilantro

½ tsp fresh ginger shredded or chopped finely
1 tsp fish sauce
1 T coconut aminos (this is fermented coconut)
½ tsp lime juice
½ sea salt
¼ tsp pepper

- Preheat oven to 350°. In a large bowl, break apart ground chicken. Measure sunflower seeds and then use a coffee grinder or mini food processor to grind them into "flour." Chop the ginger, garlic, scallions, Swiss chard (or spinach) and cilantro. Shred the carrot with the fine side of the grater. Mix all these veggies into the meat with your hands and then add the sunflower seed flour. Last, add the fish sauce, coconut aminos, lime juice, salt and pepper. When well mixed, roll into 1 inch balls. Place on a baking sheet covered with foil and bake for 20 minutes.
- This recipe can easily be doubled or tripled and you can freeze the meatballs before they are cooked on baking sheets and then transfer into a one gallon Ziploc bag and keep in freezer until use. Freezing them on the sheets before putting them in bags will keep them separated until use. Remember to do the opposite to thaw them; pull them out of the freezer, place on baking sheet and allow to defrost before baking.
- If you like sauce, you can pour warm coconut milk over them.
- Serve with a salad made of kale and mixed greens, chopped cucumber, 1 pickle chopped, ½ C green olives (without pimento), ½ C black olives, ¼ C olive oil, 2 tsp apple cider vinegar and salt and pepper. Lemon substitutes well for the vinegar if you prefer.

Chicken Meatballs with Steamed Veggies, page 42

Mustard Chicken with kale and carrots, page 45

MUSTARD CHICKEN

This chicken requires a little bit of planning…the chicken needs to sit in the marinade for a few hours to give the best flavor.

2 boneless skinless chicken breasts (split and trimmed)
¼ C white balsamic vinegar
¼ C organic olive oil
3 cloves of garlic, minced
2½ T organic brown mustard
1 tsp salt
½ tsp pepper

- You should have 4 pieces of chicken once you trim the breasts and split them evenly. They will brown better in the pan if they are all of even thickness and flat. Salt and pepper your chicken.
- In a 2 C measuring cup, mix the balsamic vinegar, oil, garlic and mustard. Put the chicken into a one gallon Zip-lock bag or a glass 8x8 pan - either will work fine. Pour the marinade mix over the chicken and seal bag and mix well to coat the chicken. Refrigerate for several hours or overnight if you thought ahead that much.
- Heat a 12 inch skillet to medium and coat lightly with coconut oil. Shake off the chicken and place the chicken in the pan, but reserve the marinade sauce.
- Brown the chicken on both sides about 3 minutes each side. Turn the heat down to low and add the marinade. Allow the chicken and sauce to simmer until slightly reduced, about 15 minutes.
- Scrape bottom of pan for the browned bits and serve.

Zucchini Boats with Ground Beef, page 47

ZUCCHINI BOATS

This is a great meal for anytime of year. It is easy on the grill or in the broiler.

4 large zucchini or 8 small.

- Cut zucchini in half lengthwise. Scoop out the middle and put aside in a bowl.
- Drizzle olive oil, sea salt and pepper inside and put the zucchini "boats" in the broiler on low for 5-6 minutes, until they soften.

Meanwhile prepare the filling:

Brown 1½ lb grass-fed ground beef

Chop the zucchini "insides" you just pulled out to make the boats and mix with the following:

1 large carrot, shredded

¼ C chopped onion

1 clove of garlic finely minced

1 tsp oregano

½ tsp fennel seeds ground with mortar and pestle

3 T fresh chopped cilantro

3 T fresh chopped parsley

½ tsp lime juice

1 tsp coconut aminos or chicken stock

- In a medium skillet, brown the ground beef on medium heat. Once the beef is cooked through, remove from the pan.
- Add veggies and simmer until soft, not soggy.
- Mix the beef and veggies together.
- Fill the Zucchini Boats with the beef and veggie mixture.
- Place under the broiler or on a grill for 5-10 minutes.
- You can melt cheese on top if you like.

I LIKE TO SERVE THIS MEAL WITH STEAMED BROCCOLI AND SAUTÉED BRUSSELS SPROUTS.

— KEENA

Raspberry Balsamic Chicken with Steamed Broccoli, page 49

RASPBERRY BALSAMIC CHICKEN

This is a quick and easy week-night chicken meal. It is super accommodating and wonderful with almost any fruit added. I have used chopped apricots in place of the berries. I have also used fresh peaches when in season. Have fun experimenting with different fruits, but keep the ratios the same on the balsamic.

4 boneless skinless chicken breasts (pound thin with mallet)
salt and pepper
½ tsp dried thyme
½ red onion, chopped finely
2 cloves of garlic chopped finely or crushed
3 T balsamic vinegar
$1/3$ C berry preserves or all fruit spread (raspberry, wild blueberry)

- Rinse chicken, pat dry, and season with sea salt, pepper and thyme. For best browning and even cooking, pound your chicken to ½ inch thickness.
- In a 12 inch skillet, pour a half-dollar sized puddle of extra virgin olive oil in your pan and heat to med-med high. Spread the oil around and add the onion and garlic to brown for 2 minutes. Then add the chicken and brown 3 minutes on each side. Cover and finish cooking the chicken until no longer pink inside.
- Remove the chicken to a plate and cover to keep warm. De-glaze the pan by pouring the 3 T balsamic vinegar into the pan and scraping browned bits of onion, garlic and chicken off the bottom of pan. Add the berry preserves, stir until warm and then remove pan from heat.
- Serve chicken with 1 T sauce over top.

TIP: Chicken breasts vary in thickness and that affects how they cook. The better contact they have with the pan, the more brown the exterior will cook in the initial contact with the hot pan. This alone yields a prettier chicken on the plate. However, the varied thickness of the breast also affects even cooking. Often the thicker part will take longer to cook leaving the thinner ends dry. So, to insure even browning and cooking, use a meat mallet with the flat end to pound out your chicken breast. You can cover the chicken with plastic wrap to avoid splatters.

MEXICAN SHREDDED BEEF

2½ lb grass-fed beef stew meat
1 T chili powder
1 tsp Real salt
1 T avocado oil
1 medium onion sliced
4 cloves of garlic
½ C chicken stock
¼ C chopped cilantro

- In a pressure cooker, heat on medium heat with avocado oil. Cut beef in 1½ inch cubes and toss beef with chili powder and salt and add to pressure cooker. Add sliced onion and garlic cloves whole. Brown beef on all sides for 3 minutes.
- Add chicken stock and set pressure cooker to high pressure. When pressure cooker reaches pressure, cook on medium heat for 20 minutes and then allow pressure to release on its own.

ROSEMARY HONEY CHICKEN

1 T rosemary chopped finely
½ C honey
¼ tsp salt
¼ C olive oil
¼ C apple cider vinegar
1 lb organic chicken of choice (breasts or thighs)

- Mix marinade in a stainless steel or glass bowl. Add chicken and allow to marinade for an hour or two.
- Heat grill to 350° and grill chicken for 10 minutes on each side, dipping in marinade when chicken is turned.

G
D
P

earthjems

CHICKEN NUGGETS

1 lb ground chicken
1 tsp onion powder
1 tsp garlic powder
½ tsp salt
¼ tsp white pepper (can omit)
2 T coconut flour
coconut oil for frying

- Mix ground chicken and spices. Roll into 1 inch balls and flatten into discs. Coat gently with coconut flour. Prepare a pan with 1 T coconut oil.
- Place nuggets in oil and cook on each side for 3-5 minutes turning only once so they stay together. Serve with a salad of mixed greens dressed with oil and vinegar.

WHITE CHICKEN CHILI

2 (14.5 oz) cans of organic Eden navy beans
½ medium jalapeño pepper, minced
2 medium poblano peppers, chopped
½ large onion, chopped
4 garlic cloves, minced
kosher salt and freshly ground black pepper
1 T ground cumin

1½ tsp ground coriander
1 tsp chili powder
4 C chicken stock
2 limes, juiced, plus lime wedges, for serving
1 whole chicken, pressure cooked or roasted
¼ C chopped cilantro leaves
tortilla chips, coarsely crushed, for topping

- Drain and rinse the canned white beans.
- In a medium bowl, mash half of the beans with a potato masher until chunky. This process will thicken the soup nicely to a chili consistency without the need for any flour to thicken the soup. Reserve the beans until needed.
- Add a bit of oil to a large soup pot and heat it over medium-high heat. Add the peppers, onions, and garlic and cook until soft and fragrant, about 5 minutes.
- Season the vegetables with salt, and pepper, to taste. Add the cumin, coriander and chili powder and continue to cook for 1 more minute to toast the spices.
- Stir in the chicken stock, and lime juice and bring to a simmer.
- Add the beans and continue to simmer for 20 more minutes. While you are simmering the soup base, prepare your chicken.

Here are a few options for how to prepare your chicken:
- You can pressure cook a whole chicken in 2 C water in a pressure cooker for 35 minutes with high pressure and then allow the pressure to release on its own. This will give you a fall-off-the-bone tender chicken and a nice juicy stock base. For more flavor in your broth, add 1 stalk of celery and 1 large carrot before you pressure cook the chicken.
- If you don't have a pressure cooker, you can roast your chicken in a 9x13 pan with about 1 C of water in the base and foil sealing the pan over the chicken.
- Roast at 350° for about 2½ hours.
- And if all else fails and you have a busy day, pick up an organic rotisserie chicken. Shred your chicken and add to the soup. Add the cilantro and finish your soup for 5 minutes at a low boil.
- Allow the soup to sit about 10 minutes to cool a bit and serve. To make it a custom chili experience, chop some fresh avocado into cubes, chop some fresh tomatoes, slice some black olives and crush some tortilla chips. Let everyone add their toppings.

earth jems

TILAPIA IN FOIL PACKETS WITH VEGGIES

4 tilapia fillets (I sometimes use frozen…I know, I know!)
1 large lemon or 2 smaller lemons, thinly sliced
2 T butter
1 zucchini, thinly sliced
8 mini bell peppers, sliced (or 1 regular bell pepper)
1 tomato, chopped
1 T capers, juice drained
1 T olive oil
1 tsp kosher salt
¼ tsp black pepper
small bunch fresh dill
salt
pepper
cooking spray
foil

- Preheat the grill to medium-high (I try to keep my temperature gauge between 400-450°). In a bowl, toss together zucchini, bell peppers, tomato, olive oil, kosher salt, and black pepper. Set aside.
- For each packet, you will need 2 large (about 20 inches long) sheets of foil, or just 1 sheet if it's the heavy duty kind. Lay your foil out and spray with cooking spray. Alternatively, you can brush them with olive oil.
- If your fish is frozen, first rinse them in cold water then pat them dry. If you're using fresh fish, you can skip this step.
- Lay one fish fillet on the foil. Sprinkle liberally with salt and pepper. Place three thin slivers of butter on top of the fish. Put two slices of lemon on top of the butter. Place a few sprigs of dill on top of that. Place ¼ of the vegetables, including capers beside the fish. Fold the long sides of the foil in toward the center and roll over to seal. Seal up the edges as well.
- Repeat with remaining fillets and vegetables.
- Place on the preheated grill, cover, and cook for 10-15 minutes. Mine took a little longer because they were frozen. To serve, carefully remove them from the grill and peel back the foil layer. Fish are done when they are white (not translucent) and flake easily with a fork. Serve in the foil packet or on plates with the sauce from the bottom of the packet.

SWEET AND SAVORY MEATLOAF

This recipe is a wonderful, flavor-ish (word courtesy of my daughter) make-over of traditional meatloaf. It combines several fresh veggies, grass-fed beef and unique seasonings. It is egg-free, dairy-free and grain-free. Get ready for a sweet and savory experience from your new, healthy meatloaf!

> 2 lb organic grass-fed, free-range ground beef
>
> Season beef with the following:
>
> ½ tsp salt, ¼ tsp pepper, ¼ tsp cinnamon, ¼ tsp nutmeg, ¼ tsp allspice
>
> 2 shallots, peeled and chopped finely
>
> 1 medium to large organic carrot, shredded finely
>
> 2-3 cloves fresh garlic minced
>
> ¼ C maple syrup
>
> ¼ C organic ketchup
>
> 1 T balsamic vinegar
>
> ¾ C chopped kale or Swiss chard (chop finely)

- Preheat the oven to 350°.
- In a large bowl, break up the ground beef and mix in the seasonings well. Add all the rest of the ingredients into the bowl and mix with your hands until well incorporated. It will take about a minute for the liquid to be equally distributed and the meatloaf to stick together. Place the meat mixture into a 9x5 loaf pan and press down the edges so the meatloaf crowns in the center and the juices can run down the sides. At this point you can cover the meatloaf and refrigerate or freeze until it is time to cook it. If putting it straight into the oven, bake at 350° for 45 minutes.
- While your meatloaf is baking, mix up the glaze:

  $^1/_3$ C maple syrup

  $^1/_3$ C apricot preserves

  1 tsp balsamic vinegar

  1 tsp mustard

- After baking 45 minutes, remove meatloaf and pour glaze on. Bake for another 30 minutes at 350°. At the end of cooking, remove the loaf pan and allow the meatloaf to cool for 10 minutes and for the meat juices to redistribute before serving.

earth jems

SPAGHETTI SQUASH WITH BACON AND PESTO

This is a very fresh and quick meal with a lot of flavor. My kids always come back for seconds of this one. The pesto gives a great raw element to the meal with spinach, pumpkin seeds and basil.

2 spaghetti squash
3 C spinach
½ C raw pumpkin seeds
2 T basil
2 cloves garlic
1 T lemon juice
1 tsp salt
½ tsp pepper
3 T olive oil
1 lb bacon or 1 lb of sausage

- Preheat oven to 375° on convection roast (or bake if you don't have the roast function).
- Cut the spaghetti squash in half lengthwise. Place face down in a 9x13 pan with about 2 inches of water. Roast (or bake) for 30-40 minutes.
- Chop the bacon and cook over medium heat until crispy.
- Making the pesto: In a blender or food processor blend raw pumpkin seeds, garlic, lemon, olive oil, spinach, basil. Blend until desired consistency. Add salt and pepper and blend again.
- When squash comes out of oven, scrape with a fork pulling the strands apart like noodles. Place in a large pasta bowl. Pour the bacon and bacon fat over the squash and mix in the pesto. Serve warm or cold.

SLOPPY JOES IN ACORN SQUASH

3 acorn squash
1 lb ground beef
2 carrots shredded
½ onion chopped
8 mushrooms chopped
4 C spinach chopped

Sauce:
¼ C organic ketchup
1 T chipotle ketchup
1 T apple cider vinegar
1 tsp yellow mustard
½ tsp celery salt
2 T brown sugar or maple syrup

- Cut the squash in half and pull out seeds. Place in a 9x13 pan (squash face down) filled with 1 inch of water. Place in oven on convection roast 350° for 30 minutes.
- Making the "Sloppy Joe" meat: place ground beef, carrot, onion, and mushrooms on medium heat for 10 minutes. Add spinach and cook until wilted.
- Mix sauce in 1 C glass measuring cup.
- Combine Sloppy Joe meat with sauce and scoop into the acorn squash halves and serve.

YOU CAN'T GO WRONG WITH A
GOOD SLOPPY JOE RECIPE –
AND IT'S EVEN BETTER THIS WAY!
–KEENA

earth jems

57

SIMPLE SHREDDED BEEF

G
D
P

2-3 lb sirloin steak
1-2 large yellow onions
½ C Imagine Organic NO chicken broth
1 tsp salt
1 tsp garlic powder
½ tsp paprika
½ tsp pepper
½ tsp white pepper
¼ tsp chili powder

- Put all ingredients in a slow cooker for 8 hours. Serve.

"

MAKE A BUCKET LIST THAT INSPIRES YOU TO DO WHAT YOU LOVE!
-KEENA

GLUTEN-FREE FRIED CHICKEN

G
D

If you love fried chicken, this will meet your cravings without the gluten!

2 lb chicken legs and thighs and 2 lb of bone-in chicken breasts
½ C brown rice flour
1 T herbs de provence (thyme, rosemary, sage)
½ C Imagine Organic NO chicken broth or vegetable broth
salt and pepper

- Remove the skin, rinse and pat dry the chicken. Sprinkle with salt and pepper. In a brown paper bag, place ½ C brown rice flour and 1 T herbs de provence. One piece at a time, shake in the bag until lightly coated. Remove from bag, dip in a bowl of almond milk and dredge in a bowl of brown rice or corn bread crumbs. I like Orgran rice crumbs. Place in a baking pan and put a pat of Earth Balance butter on top. Bake at 350° for 45 minutes.

Gravy: Use 2 C Imagine Organic NO chicken broth or your favorite organic GF chicken stock and 1T arrowroot starch. Whisk together and heat until bubbly and thickening.

PINEAPPLE CHICKEN DELIGHT

2 organic chicken breasts
1 T olive oil
1 T Earth Balance butter
7 celery lengths
2 green onions
2 large carrots
¼ green cabbage
¼ red bell pepper
1 yellow squash
1 T fresh cilantro chopped
½ fresh pineapple
3 T coconut aminos
½ tsp fresh or dried lemon peel
1 T honey
2 T pineapple juice
salt and pepper

- Cut the chicken into small cubes. On a separate cutting board: chop celery, green onions, carrots, cabbage, red bell pepper, yellow squash all into bite-size squares. Finely chop the fresh cilantro. Chop pineapple into bite-size pieces.
- Place oil and butter in a large skillet or wok. Heat to medium. Add chicken chunks and brown for 2 minutes stirring often.
- Add the carrots and celery and keep cooking on medium for 2 more minutes. Add the rest of the vegetables and the pineapple.
- Simmer on medium with lid on for 5-8 minutes until veggies are tender/crisp.
- Add 3 T coconut aminos, lemon peel and salt and pepper to taste. Serve piping hot on its own or over steamed rice!

PALEO CHILI

2 lb ground beef
1 onion
3 cloves garlic
1 red pepper
1 C carrots diced
1 C celery diced
1 rutabaga diced
1 sweet potato diced
1 jalapeño
1 28 oz can tomatoes
1 14.5 oz can diced tomatoes
1 15 oz can tomato sauce
3 T chili powder
1 T oregano
1 T basil
2 tsp cumin
1 tsp salt
1 tsp pepper
1 tsp onion powder
½ tsp cayenne powder
4 pieces of bacon
1 avocado diced

- In slow cooker on sauté setting, cook garlic and onion with ground beef while you chop your veggies. Toss all the veggies into the chili and set slow cook low for 4 hours. Serve into soup bowls and top with crispy bacon and chopped avocado.

CREAMY THAI-INSPIRED CHICKEN

This is an amazingly creamy and saucy dish for those of us that miss dairy-based sauces.
Serve this over brown rice pasta or Thai style rice noodles.

1-2 acorn squash, roasted
1½ lb chicken thighs
1 head of broccoli
3 green onions
½ C canned coconut milk
¼ C almond butter
1 T coconut aminos
1 T sweet chili sauce
1 tsp sesame oil
1 tsp honey
1 clove garlic
¼ tsp salt
1 T avocado oil
2 T chopped cilantro
handful roasted, salted cashews

- Start by removing seeds from squash and roasting in 1 inch of water. Oil a skillet and cook chicken thighs on medium heat, covered. Add chopped green onion to chicken while it is cooking. Cook 5 minutes per side.
- Clean and chop the broccoli into bite-size pieces. Mix the sauce in a 2 C measuring cup: coconut milk, almond butter, coconut aminos, sweet chili sauce, sesame oil, honey and garlic clove. When the chicken is done, salt and pepper it, then remove from pan. Chop chicken finely.
- Add the broccoli to the hot empty skillet and fry for 1 minute. Add a bit of water to create steam and cover. Add the chicken back into the pan with the broccoli and add the sauce. Scoop in the roasted squash and stir until squash is incorporated into the sauce.
- Simmer and serve.

ITALIAN MEATLOAF

1 lb grass-fed ground beef
1 yellow onion, diced
1 roasted red pepper, diced
¼ C tomato sauce
1 egg, whisked
¾ C almond flour
1 tsp dried basil
1 tsp dried thyme
1 tsp dried parsley
salt and pepper, to taste
olive oil, for sautéing

For the sauce:
¾ C tomato sauce
1 tsp dried basil
1 tsp dried thyme
1 tsp dried parsley
salt and pepper, to taste
fresh basil, chopped (to top-optional)

- Preheat oven to 400°. Place a medium skillet over medium heat and add 1-2 T of olive oil. Then add your onions and roasted red pepper to the pan.
- Cook until onions have become soft and translucent. Once they are done cooking, add them to a bowl along with the rest of the ingredients for your meatloaf and use your hands to mix it all together. Press ingredients into a bread pan and bake for 35-40 minutes.
- Once your meatloaf is almost done cooking, add your sauce ingredients to a saucepan to heat up until slightly bubbly. Let meatloaf cool slightly then add sauce on top. Top with some fresh basil. Then eat it all up!

www.earthJEMS.com

GRILLED CHICKEN MEDITERRANEAN

This is a brilliant and simple recipe. It gives beautiful color to your plate. It also packs a briny, flavorful and nutritious punch. Enjoy when tomatoes are fresh out of your garden. Or even with canned tomatoes in the winter when you crave that taste of summer!

1 C cherry or grape tomatoes
16-18 large Kalamata olives, pitted and halved
3 T capers, rinsed
2 T olive oil
2 lb boneless, skinless chicken breasts or thighs

- Season chicken with oregano, basil, garlic powder, dried lemon peel, sea salt and freshly ground black pepper. Heat grill to 350°(med-low). Place chicken on grill and grill 5-10 minutes on each side until done. Toss tomatoes, olives, capers, and 2 tsp olive oil in a bowl. Put into a grill pan lined with non-stick aluminum foil. Grill veggies for 10 minutes or until soft and hot. Top chicken with 2 T of tomato mixture and serve.

FOR TENDER CHICKEN ALWAYS GRILL IT SLOWLY AT 350 DEGREES ON YOUR GRILL. CHICKEN DOES NOT SEAR ON HIGH HEAT LIKE STEAK, YOU JUST END UP WITH THE OUTSIDE OF THE CHICKEN BECOMING HARD AND DRY. GRILLING SLOW AND LOW WILL STILL GIVE YOU NICE GRILL MARKS, WHILE ENSURING THE TENDER, DELICIOUS CHICKEN YOU WANT.

earth jems

DUMPLINGS

Here is a recipe for those times in the winter when you need to have something comfort food oriented. These definitely don't have a lot of nutrition, but cooked in chicken stew they will make you feel great!

½ C white rice flour
^{1}/3 C cornmeal
½ tsp baking soda
½ tsp baking powder
½ tsp salt
3½ T Earth Balance butter, melted
^{1}/3 C non-dairy milk of choice (I use unsweetened almond)
1 T sugar
½ tsp xanthan gum

Prepare the dumpling dough:

- Combine flours, baking powder, baking soda, salt, xanthan gum, and sugar. Mix with a fork. Now add the melted butter. Slowly pour in the milk while mixing.
- A soft dough should form, you should be able to tear off a piece and mold it into a ball.
- Drop dough balls into your almost-boiling chicken soup/stew.
- The dumplings take about about 10-15 minutes to cook.

THAI VEGETABLES WITH GROUND BEEF

This is a very quick and easy meal that can use any or all of your favorite vegetables. The canned coconut milk makes a wonderful, creamy sauce and melds the flavors nicely.

Fresh veggies:
- Brussels sprouts
- asparagus
- mushrooms
- Swiss chard
- leek
- zucchini or yellow squash
- 1 tsp Thai seasoning
- 1 tsp cumin
- 1 clove crushed garlic
- 1 lb lean buffalo (cooked)
- 1 can coconut milk

- Brown meat and set aside. Chop all the veggies, add a bit of olive oil to a pan and stir fry veggies-tender crisp. Remove veggies and set aside.
- Pour ½ can coconut milk into saucepan. Add veggies, meat, and remaining spices, mix all together and cook 5 minutes for spices to meld.

CURRY GROUND BEEF MEATBALLS

Meatballs:

2 lb grass-fed ground beef
½ yellow onion
¼ C pine nuts
1 T parsley
2 tsp garam masala
½ tsp ginger
salt and pepper to taste
1-2 T coconut oil for cooking

Sauce:

1½ - 2 C canned coconut milk
(the more the better)
1 C organic chicken broth
½ onion, diced
1 tsp red curry paste
2 tsp garam masala
1 tsp fresh grated ginger

- Place meat in large stainless steel bowl and break the meat apart. Finely dice the onion and parsley and add to meat. Pulse pine nuts in a small chopper or food processor until coarsely chopped and then add to meat mixture. Add garam masala, ginger and salt and pepper to meat also. Mix with your hands until well incorporated.
- In a large skillet, heat coconut oil. Using your hands, form meatballs of desired size and brown in the skillet for 2 minutes on each side. Combine the sauce ingredients in a separate bowl and stir with a whisk until the curry paste and coconut milk are well combined. Pour into the meatball pan and bring to a boil, simmering uncovered for about 10 minutes.
- Serve over steamed rice or paleo style by itself with no grain. Also pairs well with some pan sautéed zucchini and yellow squash.

CITRUS-MANGO SPICY TILAPIA AND KALE

This recipe is flexible, so choose any fish and any type of greens.

5-6 tilapia fillets
1-2 T Moroccan spices
1-2 bundles of kale, chopped or torn apart
1 mango, thinly sliced
3-4 garlic cloves, minced
4-6 T olive oil
   (or other oil of your choice)
2 oranges, halved
2 limes, halved
2 lemons, halved

- Get out a large sauté pan and a medium pan. If you have two large ones, that would work even better! Also pull out a shallow bowl or plate to put your spices on.
- Heat up 2-3 T of olive oil under medium-high heat in your large pan. While the pan heats, add spices to your bowl and lay your fish in the bowl to completely cover both sides in the spices.
- Add fish to hot greased pan and let cook for about 3-4 minutes. When you flip the fish to cook on the second side, squeeze half a lemon, lime and orange directly on top of the fish and add your sliced mango. Cook another 1-2 minutes. Mix around a bit to season the mango with some of the leftover spices.
- While your fish cooks, add your remaining olive oil to your second pan and add your minced garlic to cook it down a bit. Once the garlic smells fragrant, add in your chopped up kale. Squeeze the other halves of your lemon, lime, and orange on top of the kale and mix around a bit with a large spoon. Once the kale is covered in olive oil and the citrus juices, add 1 tsp of water and cover to help the kale cook down. Keep an eye on it and mix it around a bit if needed as it tends to burn quickly if left alone.
- Once the kale is sautéed and fish is done cooking, add your kale to a plate and top off with a tilapia fillet with a few slices of mango on top.

earth jems

CHICKEN ENCHILADA CASSEROLE

This is a grain-free, dairy-free enchilada bake. Yummy!

1 lb chicken shredded
1 can red enchilada sauce (Check the label to make sure this is gluten-free!)
1 can diced green chilies
¼ onion
2 cloves garlic
¼ tsp chili powder
¼ tsp oregano
salt and pepper
3 eggs, whisked
¼ C chopped cilantro

Topping:

chopped tomatoes
chopped black olives
shredded lettuce

- Preheat oven to 350°. Grease a 8x8 glass baking dish. Mix all the ingredients and pour into baking dish. Bake for 45 minutes.
- Meanwhile, toss tomatoes, olives and lettuce. Remove casserole from oven and cut into 6 pieces. Top with tomatoes, olive and lettuce mixture.

CHICKEN WITH BRUSSELS SPROUTS AND MUSTARD SAUCE

This dish has a nice sauce for those of you that love saucy dishes.
The flavors are rich without being overpowering. Serves 4-6.

2 T olive oil
4 chicken breast halves, organic
½ tsp salt
¼ pepper
¾ C chicken broth
¼ C apple cider or apple juice
2 T Dijon mustard
2 T coconut oil
1 T chopped flat leaf parsley
1 lb Brussels sprouts, trimmed and halved

- Heat oven to 450°.
- In an oven proof pan, heat 1 T oil, sprinkle salt and pepper on chicken and put in skillet for 3 minutes each side.
- Place chicken in the oven and bake at 450° for 9 minutes. Remove chicken from pan and keep warm.
- Add ½ C broth and cider, bring to a boil and de-glaze the pan. Reduce heat to low and simmer until thickened. Whisk in mustard, coconut oil and parsley.
- Meanwhile, pan fry Brussels sprouts 2 minutes, add ¼ C broth and steam for 10 more minutes.
- Mix sprouts and chicken and serve with sauce.

BRAISED CHICKEN AND MANGOS

This is a great year-round dish that can easily be served with a salad in the summer or with rice and steamed veggies in the winter. Serves 6.

1 ½ T olive oil or for a tropical flavor, use coconut oil

1 large shallot chopped

2 lb boneless, skinless chicken thighs, cut into 2 inch pieces

4 cloves of garlic, chopped or sliced thinly

1 tsp sea salt

1 C chardonnay or white cooking wine

½ C Imagine Organic NO chicken broth

2 ripe mangos, cut into 1 inch chunks (substitute: frozen mango chunks)

- Heat oil in a large skillet over med-high heat. Add chopped shallot and stir until golden brown, about 7 minutes. Add chicken and garlic, cook until browning and juices are cooking off, about 15 minutes more. Add wine and cook, scraping pan to remove browned bits and reduce to half. Stir in broth and mangos. Cover and reduce heat and simmer until chicken is cooked through and mangos start to break down, about 20 minutes. Enjoy!

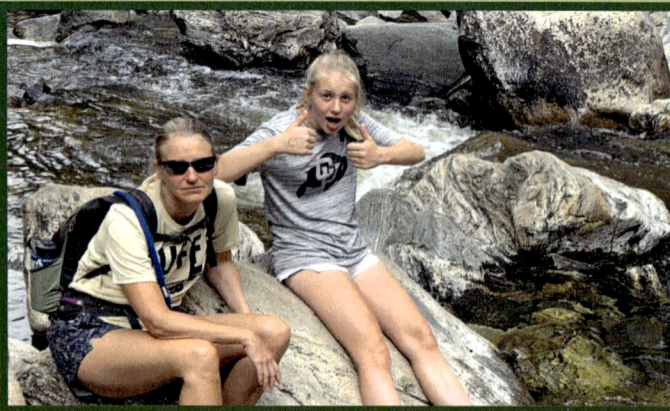

“

WEAR YOURSELF OUT IN NATURE.
-KEENA

CHICKEN POT PIE

Chicken Pot Pie is a classic comfort food. Choose different veggies each time for a new dish. Enjoy it again with this fabulous GF version!

Pot Pie Filling

2 carrots, peeled and diced

2 parsnips, peeled and diced

1 yellow onion, diced

1 small bunch fresh collards, any other green will work too (4-5 C chopped, stems removed)

8 oz mushrooms, chopped

1-2 T fresh thyme

1 lb chicken breasts (or thighs or a mix)

4 T oil

3 C chicken stock

1 T potato starch (or Tapioca or Arrowroot starch)

salt and pepper to taste

For Crust

4 egg whites

1 C almond flour

1 tsp baking powder

1 tsp salt

$1/3$ C butter (I use butter, but think non-hydrogenated palm shortening or coconut oil would work well too.)

- In a large soup pot with a lid, heat your oil over medium-high heat, then add your diced chicken. You want your pot to be pretty hot. You need to let it cook untouched for a bit to get it a little brown. Test by peeking under a piece. When you've reached the desired brown-ness, go ahead and stir and finish cooking the chicken until done. This should take 4-6 minutes. Remove the chicken from your pot and set aside.
- Add the remaining 2 T oil and all of your peeled, diced veggies (carrot, parsnip, onion, collards, mushrooms, thyme) to your pot and cover. Stir occasionally until all vegetables are cooked through and collards are almost finished cooking. Your collards should be wilted down and soft with a slight bite still to them. This will take 10-15 minutes. Now add the stock. Bring this up to a simmer and let the veggies and collards cook a little longer, about 5 minutes. Add your chicken back in. The potato starch is going to be your thickener. To prevent it from clumping, add 1 T of starch to a small bowl along with 1-2 T water. Whisk or stir with fork until all lumps are gone and then add to the pot. Stir this through and reduce the heat until the mixture reaches a thickness that looks right for pot pie filling.
- Remove this from the heat and add to any oven-safe bake-ware (Pyrex, stoneware, etc.). You could use ramekins and make individual pot pies here. Try to choose a size that will be filled to the brim by your mixture. However, this is not essential.

For your biscuit topping:

- Let the butter (or palm shortening/coconut oil) get slightly softened and add it to your mixer bowl with the almond flour, salt and baking powder. Mix until evenly distributed. If you don't have a mixer, do this with a fork. Now add your egg whites to the mix and stir to combine. Keep this mixture in the fridge if you make it ahead. When you're ready to bake just top your pot pie veggie mixture (ramekins or other) with the dough. Bake at 400° for 12-15 minutes until the crust top is golden brown.

AWESOME ASIAN NOODLE SALAD

This is one of my favorite salad dinners. It has a mellow, almost sweet taste so the kids love it as well. Feel free to add more veggies if you want to experiment.
Makes 6 servings.

3 chicken breasts, cut into bite-size pieces
1 tsp lemon grass (dried)
½ lb snap peas, cut in thirds
1 large cucumber, chopped in bite-size chunks
½ head of organic iceberg lettuce, finely chopped
½ head of romaine, chopped
5 green onions, sliced
Eden thin rice noodles, cooked and rinsed in cool water
½ C raw cashew halves toasted (or toasted pine nuts)
optional ingredients: tomato, apple, pineapple

- Stir fry the chicken in 1 tsp sesame oil or other high heat oil over med/high heat, chopping finely with a wooden utensil as it cooks. Cook about 5 minutes. Add sea salt and pepper and 1 tsp lemon grass. Remove chicken from skillet and keep warm. Add a bit more oil, green onions and snap peas. Stir fry on high until tender, stirring or tossing constantly.
- Combine chicken, rice noodles and stir fry veggies. Pour over the washed, chopped greens and cucumber in a large salad bowl. Mix dressing (recipe below) and enjoy!

Dressing:
3 T olive oil
1 T toasted sesame seed oil
2 T Bragg's apple cider vinegar
2 tsp rice wine vinegar
2 T maple syrup

THIS MEAL KEEPS WELL IN THE FRIDGE OVERNIGHT FOR LUNCH THE NEXT DAY!

- Mix dressing well with whisk and pour over salad, tossing well.

ASIAN TURKEY MEATBALLS
SERVED WITH CUCUMBER CHOP SALAD

½ C rice breadcrumbs (you can omit)
1½ lb ground turkey thighs
3 scallions, white and green parts separated
   and thinly sliced
$^1/_3$ C chopped fresh cilantro leaves
¼ C finely shredded carrot
2 tsp fish sauce
4 tsp coconut aminos
1 tsp Thai seasoning
1 tsp lime juice
1 large garlic clove, minced
lime wedges, for serving

Cucumber Chop Salad:
2 tomatoes, chopped
1 cucumber, cut lengthwise chopped
1 large kosher dill pickle
½ C green olives
½ C black olives
¼ C parsley
¼ C olive oil
½ head of iceberg lettuce, chopped finely
juice of 1 lemon
salt and pepper to taste

- Preheat oven to 450°. In a medium saucepan, bring 1½ C salted water to a boil. Add rice, stir, and return to a boil. Cover, reduce to a simmer, and cook until rice is tender, about 15 minutes. Remove from heat. Let stand, covered, 5 minutes.
- Meanwhile, in a medium bowl, combine breadcrumbs and 3 tsp water. Let stand 5 minutes. Add turkey, shredded carrot, scallion whites, cilantro, fish sauce, hot-pepper sauce, sugar, garlic, and 1½ tsp salt. Gently mix to combine and form into 12 meatballs.
- In a large non-stick skillet, heat 1 tsp oil over medium-high. In batches, brown meatballs on all sides, 10 minutes total (add up to 1 tsp oil as needed). Transfer to a rimmed baking sheet and bake until cooked through, 10 minutes. Serve meatballs with rice, scallion greens, and lime wedges.
- Serve with cucumber chop salad.

earth jems

ALMOND CHICKEN

This is a great Asian-inspired dish with a lot of flavors and textures going on.

4 oz raw almonds, leave whole or chop coarsely
2 T olive oil
½ C chopped sweet yellow onion
²/₃ C chopped celery
½ C chopped mushrooms of choice
1 can water chestnuts
1 can hearts of palm
2 T coconut aminos or wheat-free tamari
½ C chicken broth (use your own stock or Imagine Organic NO chicken broth)
salt and pepper to taste

- Saute almonds in oil over medium heat, stirring until brown. Remove almonds. Add onion and celery, sauté until soft and translucent. Add mushrooms and sauté 3 more minutes. Add almonds and remaining ingredients, cook until hot.
- Serve over shredded chicken. I make a whole roasted chicken in the pressure cooker. If you choose to do that, put chicken in pot with 2 C water, 1 carrot and 1 stalk celery, season with salt and pepper. Lock pressure cooker and cook for 30 minutes from time it reaches pressure rocking steadily. Turn off heat and allow cooker to set until pressure drops. Remove chicken and de-bone and shred. Strain the broth for stock to use in almond recipe above.
- Serves 4-6.

BEEF AND VEGGIES

This is an easy lunch or one pot dinner. It can all be cooked together the way it is written below. Or, if you want a very creative pretty presentation, you can cook the zucchini and yellow squash as noodles cutting them lengthwise and thinly. Then you can plate them like noodles and put the beef and other veggies on top.

1 ½ lb of grass-fed ground beef
1 bag of frozen butternut squash
1 large carrot, chopped into small pieces or shredded
½ sweet onion
1 clove of garlic
2 stalks celery
1 large yellow squash
1 large zucchini squash
½ C Imagine Organic NO chicken broth or chicken stock
½ tsp oregano
1 tsp dried fennel seeds
1 tsp sea salt
½ tsp pepper

- Start with a large 12 inch deep dish skillet. Add a drizzle of olive oil and begin browning the ground beef. Add the frozen butternut squash and mix in as the beef browns.
- The butternut squash will completely break down and create a nice binding sauce as everything is added.
- Chop or shred a large carrot, chop ½ onion finely, 1 clove of garlic smashed, chop celery in small cubes. Cube the yellow squash and the zucchini squash. Add the veggies as soon as the meat is browned and the butternut squash is broken down. Add the broth or stock. Sauté for about 5-10 minutes until tender. Add the herbs and stir into the mixture.
- Serves about 5-6.

GRILLED CHOPS WITH MINT

1½ C fresh mint
½ flat leaf parsley
2 T olive oil
2 T chicken stock or water
1½ T Bragg's apple cider vinegar
2 tsp shallots finely chopped
2 cloves garlic, minced
½ tsp sea salt
½ tsp fresh ground pepper
8 (4 oz) lamb loin chops

- In a food processor, combine mint, parsley, oil, chicken stock, shallot, garlic, salt and pepper. Pulse until blended.
- Heat your grill pan to med-high. Sprinkle salt and pepper on lamp chops. Coat the grill pan with avocado oil. I use avocado oil in this application because it can withstand the high heat of the grill pan. Cook lamb 5 minutes each side. Let chops rest, covered so the juices re-distribute. Serve with the fresh mint sauce.
- Complete the meal with mashed cauliflower and roasted brussels sprouts.

GAIN WISDOM FROM OTHERS, AND USE IT FOR YOUR WELL-BEING.

-KEENA

ISRAELI MEATBALLS

I had the opportunity to travel through Israel with my family and was blown away by all of the wholesome, fresh food and dedication to healthy eating, usually kosher. It inspired me to come up with this favorite recipe that reminds us of our awesome time in that area of the world. It's delicious and goes really well with the Cucumber Salad (page 29).

2 lb meat (I use 1 lb grass-fed beef and 1 lb organic ground lamb)
1 onion, chopped or grated
1 tsp garlic powder
½ tsp sea salt (I use Real Salt.)
black pepper to taste
1 tsp fresh chopped parsley
1 tsp coriander
1 tsp cumin
½ tsp ginger
small handful of pine nuts, chopped
2 cage-free organic eggs, beaten (optional)

- Mix all the ingredients with your hands and press lightly into balls. They can be large or small. Just make them all about the same size so your cooking time will be the same.
- Prepare your skillet with 1 T of olive oil and heat to medium. Place the meatballs in skillet and brown lightly. Add about ¼ C water and steam them for about 5-10 minutes until just cooked through. This will make them very moist and tender.
- If the ground lamb flavor stretches you too much or is too "gamy," use less or just use all beef or bison.

Variations: Feel free to add extra veggies. Sometimes I grate a small zucchini, carrot, or parsnip into the meat ball mixture.

GREAT GREENS

How do you make all the leafy greens that are so good for you taste great? This is one of my family and client's favorite ways to enjoy green vegetables. Make with or without meat for a side dish or a complete meal.

1 bunch of collard greens
1 bunch of flat-leaf parsley
1 lb spinach
1 bunch of rainbow Swiss chard
1 lb Brussels sprouts
1 bunch kale
½ lb mushrooms
½ yellow sweet onion
1½ T Bragg's apple cider vinegar
2 tsp shallots finely chopped
4 cloves garlic, minced
½ tsp sea salt
½ tsp fresh ground pepper
1 C vegetable broth
½ lb turkey bacon or chicken sausage
2 T oil

- Start with a large skillet or Dutch oven and 2 T of oil. I like to use Chosen Blend for high heat.
- Heat your skillet to medium. Add minced garlic and chopped onion. Cook until onion is translucent.
- While this is cooking, chop all of your greens.
- If you want protein, add turkey bacon or sausage and cook for 2 more minutes.
- Add mushrooms and Brussels sprouts. Continue to sauté for 2-3 more minutes.
- Add all the greens, cover and allow to wilt for 3-5 minutes before stirring.
- Stir, season with salt and pepper.
- For an extra "punch" you can add red pepper flakes.
- Serve warm.
- This also makes great leftovers either hot or cold.

Roasted Kabocha, page 86

VEGGIES

EARLY MORNING VEGGIE HARVESTING ON A RAINY DAY WITH OUR ORGANIC FARM FRIENDS.
-KEENA

Veggies are the most important part of our regular diet for healthy living!

SUPREME CAULIFLOWER AND CARROTS

Creamy foods can be comforting. This fits the bill, but provides a great punch of nutrition instead of starchy mashed potatoes. It is sweet because of the carrots and pairs well with GF pan-fried chicken (page 58).

1 head of cauliflower
4 medium carrots
1 small sweet onion
2 cloves of garlic
1 T fresh rosemary
1 T fresh thyme
2 T olive oil
salt and pepper

- Cut the cauliflower into small florets. Peel and chop the carrots. Steam the cauliflower and carrots until soft.
- Meanwhile, chop onion, garlic, rosemary and thyme. Place in a skillet with a small bit of olive oil. Sauté until onion is translucent. Season with salt and pepper and set aside.
- In a food processor, blend the cauliflower and carrots. Add in the onion/herb mixture. Season again with salt and pepper to taste.

"
"KEEP A GOOD ATTITUDE AND EAT YOUR VEGGIES!"
–KEENA

GRILLED VEGGIES

½ lb asparagus
1 head of broccoli
1 yellow squash
1 zucchini
1 yellow onion
1 T chopped parsley
1 tsp sea salt
½ tsp ground black pepper
¼ C olive or coconut oil

- Chop veggies into bite-sized pieces. Mix with olive oil, salt and pepper.
- Place in a grill basket on the grill at 350° for 15-20 minutes.

SUCCULENT SAUTÉED GREENS

This dish is a winner! Not everyone loves greens, but these greens seem to change a lot of minds. The smoky flavor of uncured turkey bacon and mushrooms take away the bitterness of the greens. There are varied textures as well because of the fresh green beans and Brussels sprouts.

½ lb of uncured turkey bacon, diced
½ T olive oil
1 shallot
2 C sliced mushrooms, mix and match for best flavors
1 C green beans, diced into about 1 inch segments
1 C Brussels sprouts, chopped 4 times across the center
1 bunch organic kale, green or lacinato
1 bunch organic green or rainbow chard
1 bunch collard greens
1 bunch spinach or 2 large handfuls baby spinach
freshly ground pepper to taste

- In a large pan cook the turkey bacon pieces and onion until the bacon starts to crisp at about medium high. Turn down the skillet to medium. Add the olive oil and let the temperature decrease a bit. Add the mushrooms, Brussels sprouts, green beans and sauté until the mushrooms are tender and release their moisture, 2-5 minutes.
- Meanwhile, chop the greens. Strip the kale from its stems and throw away the stems. Strip the Swiss chard from its stems, but chop the stems into 1 inch pieces. Immediately add the stems to the cooking pan. Now chop the kale and Swiss chard coarsely into bite-size pieces. Chop the spinach as well. Put all the greens into the pan and cover. Allow greens to wilt for about 2 minutes. Open the pan and turn, re-cover and allow to cook for 2 more minutes.
- Add sage and pepper and cook for another 1-2 minutes or until the greens are tender. YUM!

RUTABAGA HASH BROWNS

I love rutabaga. It is an almost unknown and a very unappreciated vegetable. Rutabaga tastes a lot like a potato, but unlike the potato, it is not a nightshade (key to know for food sensitivities!). It can be easily substituted for the potato in many dishes. So, if you miss breakfast potatoes, try this hash brown!

2 medium rutabagas, grated to yield about 2-3 C (you can make as much as you want!)
½ finely chopped yellow onion
olive oil or Earth Balance for frying (or bacon grease if you have it)
salt and pepper to taste
a little parsley chopped up for some color

- In a medium-sized skillet, add butter to melt, then add everything else and fry to taste.
- Serve with bacon and eggs.

earth jems

ROASTED KABOCHA AND ACORN SQUASH

This is a fun and easy way to eat winter squash. So in the winter, roast away in your oven, but even in the summer you can enjoy this grilled instead. Oh, and eat the skin, cooked this way it is delicious (and healthy, of course!).

1 large kabocha squash
1 large acorn squash
salt
pepper
olive oil

- Preheat oven to 375°. Slice the squash in half and scoop out seeds. Turn the squash on its side and slice half moon slices about ¼ to ½ inch thick. Repeat with all the squash. Place in a large stainless steel bowl and gently stir to coat with olive oil, salt and pepper.
- Convection roast at 375° for 20 minutes. Or lay out on the grill with tongs in a single layer and grill at 375° for 10 minutes on each side.

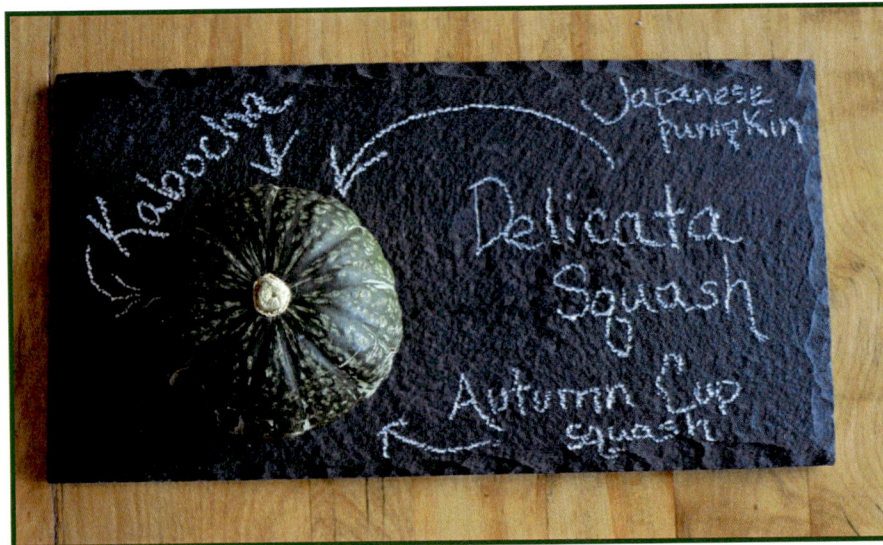

www.earthJEMS.com

GINGER/LEMONGRASS TEA STEAMED VEGETABLES

This is any easy twist on steamed veggies. It gives you a new flavor without any added fat. It is amazingly tasty for just infusing the cooking water.

5 C water
2 inch piece fresh ginger root
5 lemon grass-ginger tea bags
salt and pepper to taste
1 head cauliflower
1 head broccoli
2 zucchini
2 yellow squash
2 C Jerusalem artichokes (aka, Sunchokes)

- Peel and slice ginger root into chunks. Wash your veggies. Cut cauliflower and broccoli into small florets. Cut zucchini and yellow squash into strips about 3 inches long. Peel and chop the Jerusalem artichokes.
- Place water in the bottom of a steamer such as a bamboo steamer or a pot for cooking pasta. Add ginger, cover and bring to a boil.
- When water boils, add tea bags to water with a pinch of salt and pepper. Remove from heat, cover pot and let tea steep for 5 minutes. Remove tea bags, return to heat and bring water back to a boil. Meanwhile, prepare steaming basket: place cauliflower and broccoli florets on the bottom of the basket. Sprinkle with salt and pepper to taste. Add zucchini and yellow squash slices, followed by the Jerusalem artichokes.
- Place basket over water, making sure that the water does not touch the base of the basket. Cover and cook for about 10 minutes, until vegetables are crisp-tender.
- These veggies do not even need butter. They have a perfectly fragrant flavor.

earth jems

GRILLED ZUCCHINI WITH OLIVE PASTE

This is a fresh and simple dish you can make ahead and take out for lunch. It can be served cold, or hot.

I USUALLY PAIR THIS RECIPE WITH SOME SHREDDED OR GRILLED CHICKEN.

½ C pitted Kalamata olives or black olives
1 clove of garlic
1 T apple cider vinegar
½ tsp sea salt
½ tsp black pepper
¼ C water
½ fresh lemon
4 medium zucchini
1 large tomato, chopped

- Slice the zucchini lengthwise into ¼ thick strips. I use a mandolin to slice, but a knife and a steady hand will work just as well. Sprinkle zucchini with salt and pepper. Drizzle lemon juice on it. Place the zucchini on a hot grill for 3 minutes per side.
- Meanwhile, in a blender place olives, garlic, vinegar, salt and pepper and water. Blend until a smooth consistency is achieved. As the zucchini comes off the grill, coat in olive paste.

"LIVING THE ADVENTURE OF LIFE INCLUDES HEALTHY EATING!"
–KEENA

www.earthJEMS.com

GINGER ROASTED CARROTS

Does it get simpler? Pop these in the oven to complete any fish or chicken dish.

    8 carrots, ¼ inch slices
    2 parsnips
    2 T orange juice
    1 T ginger
    2 tsp olive oil
    ½ tsp sea salt
    ¼ black pepper
    ½ tsp orange zest

- Preheat oven to 400°. In a 9x13" baking dish place all the ingredients and stir.
- Cover the dish with foil (shiny side down to reflect the heat back down) and bake for 20 minutes.

G
D
P
V

KALE CHIPS

These are a fun, delicious and easy snack.

    1 bunch of kale cleaned, dried
    1 T avocado oil
    ½ tsp garlic powder
    $^1/_8$ tsp cayenne powder
    ¼ tsp chili powder
    1½ T nutritional yeast
    ¼ tsp pink salt
    ¼ tsp cumin
    1 T almond butter
    1 T warm water

- Remove the ribs from the kale. Chop the kale into bite-sized pieces. Mix the almond butter, water and spices.
- Put everything in a bowl and mix with your hands to coat the kale leaves with mixture.
- Place on a baking tray spread single thickness. Bake at 300° for 7-9 minutes. Watch closely.

G
D
P
V

CARROT SALAD

A simple, fresh carrot salad combines tender cooked carrots with the crunch of pepitas (or almonds). The freshness of the ginger and cilantro brings out the flavors in asian cuisine or grilled proteins. Serve this dish with Asian Turkey Meatballs (page 73), or grilled meat.

2 lbs carrots
3 T olive oil
2 T lemon juice
1 tsp grated ginger
1 tsp honey
½ C chopped cilantro
½ small red onion
½ C toasted pepitas or almonds, salted lightly as toasting

- Wash, peel and slice the carrots thinly. I use a mandolin to get even thickness to my carrot slices. In a large sauce pan bring salted water to a boil. Add sliced carrots and cook for 5 minutes until tender.
- Whisk together the olive oil, lemon juice, grated ginger, and honey for the dressing. When the carrots are tender, drain and toss with the dressing, cilantro, onions, and toasted pepitas or almonds.

"STICK YOUR HEAD OUT THE WINDOW AND LET THE WIND BLOW THROUGH YOUR HAIR!"
                                                        -KEENA

CABBAGE AND LEEK PANCAKES

These are a delicious alternative to potato pancakes. They are quick and easy to make and go well with a dinner of fried chicken (page 58) and gravy*. It is a great healthy comfort food alternative.

G
D
P
V

3 C thinly shredded organic green cabbage

2 organic leeks

¼ C GF flour

½ tsp fine sea salt

¼ tsp ground black pepper

2 eggs, beaten

Earth Balance soy free butter spread

- Shred about ½ of a cabbage. You can also shred it in a food processor. Chop the leeks into half lengthwise and then in half lengthwise again. Then chop cross-ways into 1 inch lengths. Then chop overall again to make them as "shredded" as you can by hand. Alternatively, place in a food processor until shredded.

- In a large bowl, toss together cabbage and leeks; squeeze firmly 4 or 5 times to wilt them slightly. Add GF flour or corn meal, salt, pepper and eggs and stir until well coated. Heat a large skillet over medium heat and melt about 1 T of Earth Balance spread.

- Working in batches, drop a generous ⅓ C of the cabbage mixture into skillet, spreading it out to make 4-inch pancakes. Put a small pat of Earth Balance butter on top of each pancake and cook, flipping once, until tender and deep golden brown, 8 to 10 minutes total. Transfer to a plate as done.

Here is a tip for a great gluten free "fried" chicken. (Also more details on page 58.)

2 lb of chicken legs and thighs and 2 lb of bone in chicken breasts

½ C brown rice flour

1 T herbs de provence (thyme, rosemary, sage)

salt and pepper

- Remove the skin, rinse and pat dry the chicken. Sprinkle with salt and pepper. In a brown paper bag, place ½ C brown rice flour and 1 T herbs de provence. One piece at a time, shake in the bag until lightly coated. Remove from bag, dip in a bowl of almond milk and dredge in a bowl of brown rice or corn bread crumbs. I like Orgran rice crumbs. Place in a baking pan and put a pat of Earth Balance butter on top. Bake at 350° for 45 min.

*Gravy: Use 2 C Imagine Organic NO chicken broth or your favorite organic GF chicken stock and 1 T arrowroot starch. Whisk together and heat until bubbly and thickening.

earthjems

BRUSSELS SPROUTS WITH APPLES

Brussels sprouts are one of our favorite veggies. This is a very delicious and delicately flavored preparation. The apples take away some of the distinct "cabbage" taste of the brussels sprouts. They are also easy to prepare and I find them to be quite filling for a veggie.

1 lb Brussels sprouts
2 large shallots
2 medium crisp, firm apples
½ C water, divided
¼ C Bragg's apple cider vinegar, divided
¼ tsp sea salt
½ tsp freshly ground black pepper
4 sprigs fresh thyme

- Rinse Brussels sprouts well, pull off any loose or yellowing leaves and trim the stem. Quarter each sprout. Set aside.
- Heat a large high-sided sauté pan over high heat. I use a 12 inch deep skillet with a lid. Add shallots to the very hot pan and cook, stirring constantly for 2 minutes. This gives a beautiful sear to your sprouts. Add apples and ¼ C water, scraping any brown bits from the bottom as the water sizzles. Reduce heat. Cook until the liquid reduces by half, about 2 minutes. Add Brussels sprouts, remaining ¼ C water, 2 T vinegar, salt and pepper. Reduce heat to medium, cover and simmer until the sprouts and apples are tender enough to be pierced all the way through with a fork, stirring occasionally, about 15 minutes.
- Uncover, stir in remaining 2 T vinegar and the leaves pulled from sprigs of thyme. Scrape any bits from the bottom of the pan as liquid sizzles and reduce until nearly gone.
- Transfer to a serving bowl with any of the remaining liquid and serve immediately.

RAW BEET, CARROT AND APPLE SALAD

Incorporating raw foods into our diets is important. Start with simple recipes like this one. It can be made quickly and my kids love to help use the hand juicer to make the dressing.

zest and juice of 1 orange
zest and juice of 1 lime
2 T Bragg's apple cider vinegar
$^1/_3$ C extra-virgin olive oil
sea salt and fresh ground pepper
1 lb beets, peeled and cut in matchsticks
2 large carrots, peeled and cut in matchsticks
1 Granny Smith apple, cored, peeled, and cut in matchsticks
1 jicama, peeled and cut in matchsticks
1 bunch flat-leaf parsley, stems removed

- In a large bowl combine orange zest and juice, lime zest and juice, and vinegar. Slowly whisk in the olive oil and season with salt and pepper to taste. Add all the veggies and serve.

"EAT TO COMPETE!"
–KEENA

BEST BOK CHOY

Bok Choy is a tasty crisp vegetable. The leaves will wilt like any green when cooked, but the stems maintain a nice crunch and juiciness to them.

8 large baby bok choy
1 T sesame oil
1 C sliced celery
1 tsp fresh grated ginger or ½ tsp powdered
2 cloves garlic, finely chopped
¼ lb fresh shiitake mushrooms
coconut aminos to sprinkle over

- Wash the bok choy thoroughly because dirt gets stuck in the stem. Chop off stems about ¼ inch up. Then chop in half lengthwise and then in ½ inch segments.
- In a large skillet, heat the sesame oil over medium-high heat. Sauté celery and ginger for 3 minutes. Add garlic.
- Add bok choy and mushrooms and sauté for 3 minutes or until vegetables are beginning to soften. The leaves will brighten and the stems will be close to fork tender (about 3-5 minutes).

GET OUTSIDE FOR FITNESS AND HEALTHY LIVING!
-KEENA

earth jems

Carrot Cake Chocolate Chip Flax Muffin, page 20

SWEET TREATS

> COMMUTING BACK HOME AFTER A LONG DAY ON THE MOUNTAIN - PROBABLY WONDERING WHAT DESSERT IS WAITING!
>
> -KEENA

Sweets can energize the soul - and they're a special treat that shows love!

Texas Sheet Cake, page 99

TEXAS SHEET CAKE

This gluten-free, dairy-free, egg-free delight is made with almond and brown rice flour.
Ground chia seeds replace the egg for a healthy, light cake with great texture.

1 C almond flour
½ C sweet rice flour
¼ C brown rice flour
¼ C arrowroot starch
4 T cocoa powder
1 C pure cane sugar, unrefined
½ tsp baking soda

$^1/_8$ tsp salt
8 T Earth Balance organic coconut spread
    (replaces butter well!)
½ C almond milk
½ C strong brewed coffee
2 T ground chia in ½ C warm water (or one XL egg)
½ tsp vanilla

- Prepare a jelly roll pan with aluminum foil or parchment paper. Preheat oven to 350°. Mix the dry ingredients in a medium bowl. In a small saucepan, heat coconut spread, almond milk and coffee until melted. Pour the warm liquid into the dry ingredients and whisk together. Pour into prepared pan. Bake for 20 minutes or until cake is springy and filled with little holes (which the icing will fill beautifully!)

While the cake is baking, make the icing:

Icing:

2 C organic powdered sugar
  (or make your own in Vitamix with cane sugar and 1 T arrowroot starch)
3 T cocoa powder
$^1/_8$ tsp salt
8 T Earth Balance organic coconut spread
3 T almond or coconut milk
½ tsp vanilla

- In a large bowl, place the powdered sugar, cocoa, salt and stir with a whisk to combine. In a small saucepan, mix coconut spread and milk. Cook on low heat until melted. Remove from heat and add ½ tsp vanilla.
- Whisk icing right into powdered sugar mixture. Pour onto the hot cake as it comes out of the oven. Spread lightly with a spatula before icing sets up. Cool to room temp or refrigerate. Cake will cut into 16 pieces. Cuts best at cool temp with a warm knife. Enjoy!

earth jems

THE BEST GLUTEN-FREE PIE CRUST

½ C almond flour
½ C brown rice flour
½ C white rice flour
¼ C millet flour
¼ C sweet rice flour
¼ C arrowroot flour
¼ C powdered sugar
½ tsp baking powder
1 tsp xanthan gum
½ tsp salt
10 T butter and shortening
   (I use soy-free Earth Balance and Spectrum Organic shortening)
½ C ice cold water (Do not just pour in!!!)

- Mix all the flours and dry ingredients. Add the butter and shortening mix and pulse in food processor if you have one. If not, I just use my pastry blender or fork and mix in until the flour is crumbly and pea sized. Slowly add ice cold water until the mixture forms into a ball completely pulling all the flours together. *I have never used all the water.* It will be slightly sticky, but not gooey. Place the ball on plastic wrap, cover completely and put into the freezer for 30 minutes until firm. Remove from freezer, divide into 2 balls and roll out each ball between plastic wrap or parchment paper.

- With fruit pie fillings, bake pie at 400° on bottom rack for 45 minutes. This will prevent the bottom of the crust from being soggy!

THE AMAZING BUNDT CAKE

3 medium, very ripe bananas, mashed
½ C applesauce
1 T vanilla extract
⅓ C extra light olive oil or grape-seed oil
2 T maple syrup
¾ C organic light brown sugar
2 C GF flour blend*
  (I use: 1 C oat flour + 1 C brown rice flour +
    ¼ cup arrowroot starch)
1 tsp baking soda
1 tsp baking powder
2 tsp ground cinnamon
¼ tsp sea salt
¾ tsp xanthan gum

*You can use a "pre-mixed" GF flour blend if you want, but then don't add xanthan gum if your mix has it.

- Preheat oven to 350°. Prepare a bundt cake pan by rubbing a little oil in it.
- Place the banana purée into a bowl. Add the applesauce, vanilla, olive oil, maple syrup, and light brown sugar. Beat for 1 minute on medium speed. In a separate large bowl, measure and combine your dry ingredients.
- Add the wet ingredients into the dry mix and beat for 2 minutes. **This step is important because you are not using eggs and you need the batter to take on air and mix very well!** Pour the batter into the prepared pan and bake in the center of a preheated oven for 40-50 minutes until done. Check the center for done-ness with a wooden pick. The toothpick should come out almost totally clean. The cake should be firm and springy to the touch and may appear slightly golden brown at the edge, yet still be moist inside.
- Cool the cake on a wire rack for 10 minutes before releasing it from the pan (by placing a serving plate on top of the cake pan and turning it upside down onto a plate). My pan is non-stick, so my cake slides right out. But if your pan is not non-stick, be sure the edges of the cake are loosened from the sides before you invert the pan. Serves 12.

THE AMAZING BUNDT CAKE (2)

Here are some fun VARIATIONS:

1. For a chocolate cake, mix ½ C cocoa in the dry ingredients and omit the cinnamon.
2. For a chocolate chip cake, mix ½ C Enjoy Life mini chips into your batter at the end of mixing for 2 minutes.
3. For a carrot cake, mix in ½ C finely shredded carrot and ½ C chopped walnuts or pecans. Also add a pinch of nutmeg, allspice, ginger (about ¼ tsp each).
4. For an apple cake, add 1 large apple, peeled and chopped. Stir apples in after 2 minutes.

You can GLAZE the cake with many combinations:

1. For a chocolate glaze: use ¼ C cocoa, 1 C powdered sugar, 2 T canned coconut milk (blend with whisk or hand mixer adding more coconut milk if necessary to get right consistency).
2. For a vanilla glaze: Use 1¼ C powdered sugar, 1 T vanilla, 2 T canned coconut milk. Again, mix to desired consistency.
3. For a cream cheese icing on the carrot cake variation, use vegan cream cheese and powdered sugar. Blend with hand mixer and add a bit of canned coconut milk if necessary to thin your icing.

MOIST AND LIGHT VANILLA CAKE

This recipe is a great choice for vegan or egg-free friends.
It is also nut-free (depending on what milk you choose).
It will amaze you with its light and fluffy texture.
Enjoy your special occasions again without worries about allergies or food sensitivities!

Chef's tip: Line the bottom of your cake pans with parchment paper. Cut the parchment paper to fit the bottom. This will insure easy cake removal for layer cakes.

1½ C sweet rice flour (can use sorghum flour or oat flour if you wish)
1½ C tapioca flour
1 C white rice flour
2 C white sugar
1 tsp sea salt
2 T baking powder
2 tsp baking soda
2 tsp xanthan gum
1 C coconut milk
2 C warm water
6 T coconut oil melted
2 T vanilla extract
2 tsp apple cider vinegar
½ C unsweetened applesauce

- Preheat oven to 375°. Measure milk into a glass measuring cup and add vinegar. Set aside.
- Whisk together all the dry ingredients.
- Add liquid to dry ingredients and mix with mixer until smooth and fluffy - about 2 minutes.
- Grease two 9 inch round cake pans, or one 9x13 pan and pour batter into pans.
- Bake cake for 35 minutes. The cake will be light brown on top and spring back when pressed lightly.

"USE YOUR CREATIVITY
TO ENJOY THE LITTLE
THINGS IN LIFE!"
—KEENA

MAYA'S ALMOND CAKE

½ C organic, unsweetened applesauce
1 T organic chia seeds, ground (measure after grinding)
2 T hot water
$1/3$ C honey
1 tsp vanilla
2 C almond flour
1 tsp baking powder
1 tsp cinnamon
¼ tsp sea salt

- Preheat oven to 350° and grease an 8×8 glass baking pan with coconut oil.
- In a large mixing bowl, beat the applesauce with the chia meal and hot water on high for 2 minutes, stopping once to scrape down the sides and bottom. Add honey and vanilla and beat until combined.
- In a small bowl, whisk together the dry ingredients: almond flour, baking powder, cinnamon, and salt. Add to the mixing bowl and beat just until incorporated. Stir once or twice with a spatula to make sure everything on the bottom is mixed in. The batter will be thick! Pour it into the prepared pan and spread it evenly with the spatula.
- Bake at 350° for 30 minutes, or until the top is golden brown and a toothpick comes out clean. Cool in pan for 15-20 minutes, then turn out onto a cooling rack and let cool completely. Cut and serve, or decorate with frosting. Enjoy!

KEY LIME COCONUT TREATS

½ C almonds
½ C cashews
1 ½ C medjool dates
zest and juice of 3 key limes
½ C coconut flakes

- Add almonds and cashews to the bowl of a food processor. Pulse until nuts are finely chopped, but not turned into a paste.
- Add the dates, juice and zest of lime and blend until combined.
- Roll into balls and roll in coconut.
- Store in refrigerator.
- A fun and delicious treat!

"SMILE – IT'S GOOD MEDICINE!"
–KEENA

BANANA CAKE

1½ C almond flour
¼ C hazelnut flour
¼ C ground flax
¼ C arrowroot starch
1 tsp baking soda
1 tsp baking powder
1½ tsp pumpkin pie spice
¼ tsp sea salt
2 T coconut flour
2 eggs
⅓ C sunflower oil
½ C light brown sugar
2 ripe bananas
2 tsp vanilla extract

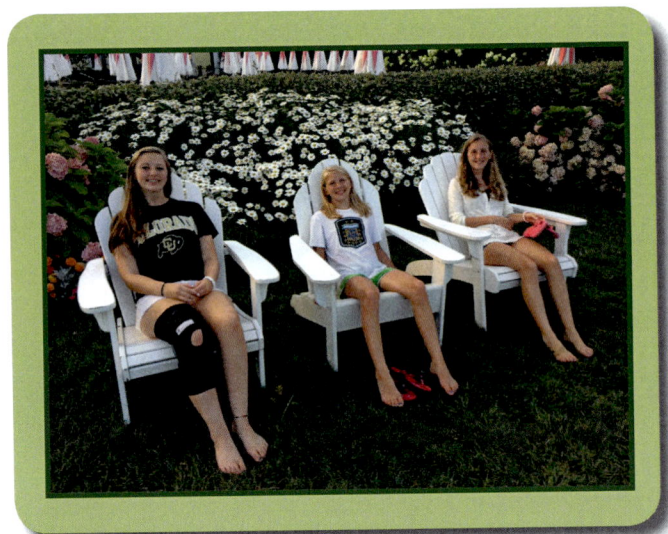

- Preheat oven to 350°. Prepare a 10x12 rimmed jelly roll pan with greased parchment paper on the bottom or use cupcake pan and make muffins. Makes 14.
- Mix all the dry ingredients in a bowl. In the mixing bowl, mix eggs, oil, sugar, bananas and vanilla. Pour batter into prepared pan and bake in preheated oven for 35 minutes.

"

"LOVE GIVES US A FRONT-ROW SEAT WITH FRIENDS AND FAMILY!"
-KEENA

GLUTEN-FREE BANANA SPLIT CAKE

1 C sweet white rice flour
¼ C arrowroot starch
½ C almond meal
2 eggs
1 C sugar
1 C chopped bananas
½ tsp xanthan gum
1½ tsp baking powder
½ tsp salt

¼ C grape-seed oil
¼ almond milk
¼ C chopped and toasted walnuts
½ C Enjoy Life mini chocolate chips
⅓ C chopped canned pineapple
1 tsp vanilla extract

- Preheat oven to 350°. Grease a non-stick 9 inch bundt cake pan with coconut oil.
- Whisk rice flour, arrowroot starch, almond meal, salt, and xanthan gum together in a bowl. In mixing bowl beat sugar and oil together for 45 seconds. Add eggs to this mixture one at a time. Next add banana and vanilla.
- Fold the flour into the mixture alternating with the ¼ C almond milk. Fold in chocolate chips, walnuts and pineapple. The batter will be thicker than a pancake batter, but not as thick as cookie dough. Pour batter into the bundt pan, smooth the top and bake for 45-50 minutes until golden brown and toothpick comes out clean. Allow to rest on wire baking rack for 20 minutes. Gently place a plate on top and flip cake pan over. The bundt cake should slide right out.

- Mix the glaze:
    2 T Earth Balance soy-free butter
    2 T almond milk
    ¼ C powdered sugar
    ½ C chocolate chips
- Melt butter and chocolate chips in double boiler or microwave. Add milk and powdered sugar and stir with a whisk. Pour over cake and serve.

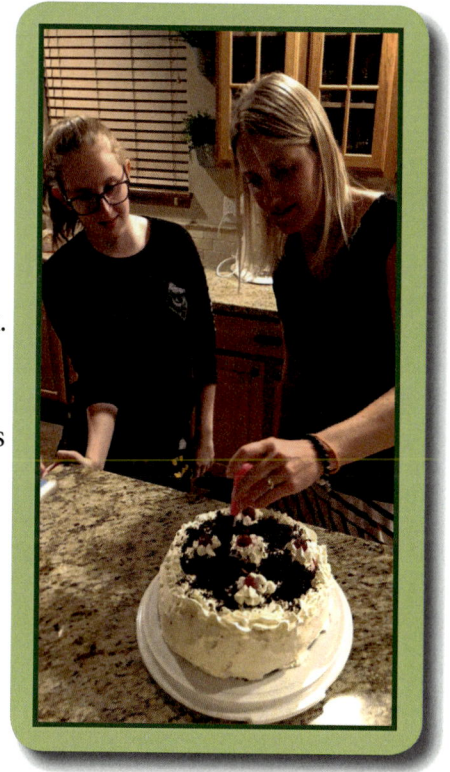

GLUTEN-FREE FRUIT AND BERRY CRISP

Crisp Topping:

½ C buckwheat flour

½ C white rice flour

$^1/_3$ C GF quick oats (if you can't tolerate oats, substitute with more GF flour mix and/or more chopped nuts)

$^1/_3$ C organic white or cane sugar

½ tsp sea salt

1 tsp ground cinnamon

½ C chopped nuts (chop first, then measure)

6-8 T melted unsalted butter, coconut oil or shortening

Filling:

4 C sliced, peeled and cored fruit (like apples, pears, peaches, nectarines and/or blueberries, blackberries)

$^1/_3$-½ C sugar or agave nectar (use more sugar or agave if the fruit is tart or if you use more than 4 C of fruit)

2 T cornstarch or any other starch like tapioca or arrowroot

- Preheat the oven to 375°. Grease a 2 to 2½ quart baking dish or deep pie dish.
- Make the crisp topping and set aside.
- Mix the fruit, sugar and cornstarch and toss gently. Transfer the fruit mixture to the baking dish and cover with the crisp topping, spreading evenly.
- Place in the oven and bake until the top is well browned and the fruit is tender when pierced with a knife, about 30-35 minutes.
- Serve with whipped cream or ice cream.

COCONUT PROTEIN BARS

½ C coconut butter, melted
2 T applesauce
2 T honey
¼ tsp coconut extract
¼ tsp vanilla
3 T protein of choice
3 T flaxseed ground
2 T raw cashews
2 T coconut flour
pinch of salt

Topping:
½ C dark chocolate chips
1 T oil

- Process the first 10 ingredients in a food processor or Vitamix blender. Process until smooth.
- Spread into an 8x8 baking dish lined with parchment paper.
- Melt chocolate and oil together and pour over the bars.
- Dust with shredded coconut.
- Freeze overnight, slice and serve.

> "LIFE IS A BEAUTIFUL MESS.
> ENJOY IT TOGETHER!"
> —KEENA

G
D
P
V

CHOCOLATE RASPBERRY TART

To make the crust:

1 C raw almonds

1 C raw pecans

$^1/_3$ C pitted medjool dates

- Blend in the food processor or Vitamix on high until a ball forms.
- Spread the ball in the bottom of a tart pan or shallow pie plate. Set aside.

Filling:

1 can of organic coconut milk (not lite)

2 T arrowroot starch

1 tsp vanilla

¼ tsp sea salt

1 C Enjoy Life mini chocolate chips or chocolate chunks

$^1/_3$ C all fruit raspberry or blackberry seedless preserves (such as Polamer All Fruit)

- In a sauce pan on medium heat, mix with a whisk the organic coconut milk, arrowroot starch, vanilla and salt. When the mixture reaches almost boiling, turn off heat and stir in the chocolate and the preserves. When melted and thoroughly combined, pour into the pie crust.
- Place in refrigerator for 2 hours to overnight (depending on how long you can stand to wait!)
- Enjoy!

"GET OUT OF YOUR COMFORT ZONE AND ADVENTURE!"

-KEENA

CHOCOLATE HEAVEN IN A MUFFIN

1¾ C GF oats
2 T ground chia seeds
½ C hot water
¾ C unsweetened organic cocoa
½ C unsweetened applesauce
1 tsp vanilla extract
¼ C almond milk
2 T sunflower oil
1 tsp apple cider vinegar
1½ tsp baking powder
1½ tsp baking soda
¼ tsp salt
½ C sugar
½ C Enjoy Life mini chocolate chips

- Use silicone baking cups, paper ones stick to the muffin!
- Preheat oven to 350°. In a blender mix all of the ingredients except for chocolate chips. After fully mixed, blend in chocolate chips.
- Scoop batter into 12 muffin cup and bake for 15-20 minutes.

CHOCOLATE COVERED COCONUT CASHEW BARS

This is a delicious, no-bake bar to keep in the refrigerator for when you have a Snicker's bar craving in the afternoon (I know I do!). They are super easy to make and are the perfect texture and temperature right out of the refrigerator.

½ C raw cashews
$^1/_3$ C melted coconut oil
1 C unsweetened coconut flakes
$^1/_3$ C honey
1 C coconut flour
1 tsp cinnamon

Topping:
½ C dark chocolate chips
1 T coconut oil melted

- In a Vitamix or food processor mix cashews, oil, coconut flakes, honey, coconut flour.
- Press into an 8x8 pan.
- Melt chocolate in microwave with coconut oil.
- Spread on top and place in freezer for an hour until set.
- Cut and serve.

TWO BITE BROWNIES

Brownies are the perfect chocolate dessert in my opinion. These can be made in that delicious two-bite style to help with portion control! Or just make a whole pan.

8 oz almond butter, at room temperature
4 T chia seeds
1 C warm water
½ C almond flour
½ C coconut flour
½ C light agave
½ C sugar
1 tsp vanilla
½ C cocoa powder
½ tsp sea salt
1 tsp baking soda
1 C Enjoy Life mini chips

- For a smooth brownie, grind chia seed in your coffee grinder.
- Mix warm water and chia together in mixing cup, stir and let sit for 15 minutes until gel forms. While you are waiting for the chia to gel, mix all ingredients except chocolate chips together until smooth. Fold in chocolate chips.
- For brownie bites, grease mini muffin tins and fill cups with 1 T brownie batter. Makes 36. Bake at 325° for 25 minutes.
- For one large brownie cake, put into a greased 9x13 pan and bake at 325° for 40 minutes.

earth jems

CHEWY OATMEAL RAISIN COOKIES

This is the perfect cookie if you love a tender, chewy oatmeal cookie. It can also be made with dried cranberries if you don't love raisins. The secret is to soak the "fruit" in boiling water while you prepare the cookie dough. The warm, moist fruit helps to steam the cookie while it is baking, locking in the moisture.

½ C coconut oil, softened

²/₃ C brown sugar

1 egg or 1 T freshly ground flax seed or chia seed mixed with ¼ C warm water,
   allow to sit for 5 minutes

1 tsp vanilla

¼ C brown rice flour

¼ C arrowroot starch

¼ C sweet rice flour

1 tsp GF baking powder

¾ tsp ground cinnamon

¼ tsp sea salt

¹/₈ tsp nutmeg

1½ C GF oats

¾ C raisins or dried cranberries (soak the raisins)

- Preheat oven to 350°. Start by soaking your raisins or cranberries in ¼ C boiling water. Then, in a large bowl, cream together the coconut oil, brown sugar, egg and vanilla until smooth and creamy.
- In a separate small bowl, whisk together the flours, baking powder, cinnamon, nutmeg, and salt. Add the dry ingredients to the wet ingredients. Blend until combined then stir in the oats and raisins (drain them first).
- Spoon approximately 1 T of dough onto the parchment covered baking sheet, leaving a 1 inch space between each cookie. Bake for 10 to 12 minutes or until golden at the edges.
- Once removed from the oven, allow to set on the hot baking sheet for 2 minutes before transferring to cooling rack.

CHERRY APRICOT CAKE

This is a very moist and delicious cake. It is completely grain-free because it uses almond flour. Tender in texture, it is almost like a sponge cake.

2 C blanched almond flour
½ tsp salt
½ tsp baking soda
½ C honey
2 eggs
1 T vanilla extract
$^1/_3$ C dried pitted cherries
¼ C apricot or peach preserves

- Preheat oven to 325°. Mix together the almond flour, salt and baking soda in a 4 C mixing bowl.
- In a smaller bowl, combine the honey, eggs and vanilla extract. Stir wet ingredients into dry until combined well. Chop the dried cherries and add to batter. Stir in the preserves.
- Pour into a 8x8 baking dish coated with cooking spray or Earth Balance soy free butter. Bake at 325° for 30-40 minutes, until golden brown and a toothpick inserted into the center of the cake comes out clean.

CASHEW CREAM FROSTING

$^2/_3$ C coconut cream
$^1/_3$ C medjool dates chopped
1 C raw cashews- soak for 1 hour first
½ tsp vanilla extract

- In food processor or blender, mix all ingredients until smooth.
- Store in refrigerator.
- Add to your favorite cake or muffins.

"LIFE IS SHORT.
MAKE EVERY MOMENT COUNT!"
–KEENA

FRUIT LAYERED BARS

1st Layer:
1 1/3 C pumpkin puree
1/3 C maple syrup
¼ C coconut oil melted
2 T ground chia seeds with 2/3 C warm water
1 tsp vanilla
¼ C coconut flour
½ tsp cinnamon
¼ tsp nutmeg
¼ tsp ground cloves
1/8 tsp ground ginger
½ tsp baking soda
½ tsp baking powder

2nd Layer:
2 C berry mix, fresh or thawed (blueberries, raspberries, cherries)
2 T honey
2 T coconut spread (Earth Balance)
1 tsp lemon juice
2 T coconut flour

3rd Layer- crumble:
½ C chopped nuts of choice (pecans, walnuts, cashews)
3 T coconut shredded
1 tsp sunflower seeds
1 T honey
sprinkle of cinnamon

- Preheat oven to 350°. For the first layer, mix the pumpkin, maple syrup, coconut oil, chia/water mix and vanilla. Beat well.
- In another bowl, whisk together coconut flour, cinnamon, nutmeg, cloves, ginger, baking soda, baking powder and salt. Pour dry ingredients into wet ingredients and mix well.
- Place parchment paper in bottom of an 8x8 baking dish and allow it to hang out on two sides. This will make it easy to pull the bars out of pan without sticking. Pour the batter into the pan and bake for 30 minutes.
- Meanwhile, mix the berries, honey, coconut spread, lemon juice together in a sauce pan. Boil and cook down for 10 minutes. Add coconut flour and remove from heat as you stir it in.
- When the pumpkin layer comes out of the oven, pour the blueberry mixture over the top. In a bowl, mix the chopped nuts, coconut, sunflower seeds, honey and cinnamon together. Spread over the blueberry mixture and put into oven for 15 more minutes.

BANANA DONUTS

This is a yummy little treat sweetened mostly with bananas to have when you or the kids need a little donut! This recipe is pretty forgiving. Use your favorite GF flour. Each GF flour has its own nutritional benefits, but in this treat, nutrition is not the most important factor. I use oat flour because I like the "oatmeal" taste it gives with the bananas. The sweet rice flour adds a sweetness, but does not give any "whole grain" nutrition.

1 T chia seed
3 T warm water
3 T milk of choice
2 bananas, mashed
3 T melted coconut oil
¼ C organic cane sugar
2 T vanilla
2 tsp cinnamon
1 C oat flour (or substitute brown rice flour or sweet rice flour)
½ tsp baking powder
½ tsp salt

- Preheat the oven to 350° degrees. In a coffee grinder, grind the chia until a fine grind.
- In a measuring, cup mix the chia and 3 T of warm water. Let it rest for a minute and it will form a gel. Stir together non-dairy milk of choice, bananas, coconut oil and vanilla. Add the chia gel and cane sugar. Mix with a hand mixer until smooth and creamy.
- Mix dry ingredients: 1 C GF flour of choice, ½ tsp baking powder, salt, cinnamon. Add dry to wet and mix on low until well combined.
- Grease a donut pan or use mini muffin tins if you don't have a donut pan. Fill the tins ¾ of the way, and bake in the oven for 8-10 minutes (for mini donuts) until just set. If you are using a large donut pan with 6 donuts shapes, you will need to bake an additional 3-4 minutes.
- Enjoy this sweet treat!!

BAKED APPLES

An old fashioned family favorite in the fall as temperatures cool and apples are at the peak of freshness. This is an easy dessert to throw in the oven while dinner is cooking for a fresh, warm treat after dinner.

6 large Gala apples
¼ C chopped walnuts
¼ C raisins
¼ C brown sugar
1 tsp cinnamon
½ tsp nutmeg
6 T maple syrup

- Preheat oven to 350°. Core the apples. Set the apples in a square baking dish.
- Mix together filling ingredients. Carefully stuff filling into the apples.
- Add about a ½ C water to the bottom of baking dish. Bake until tender, 30-35 minutes.

APPLESAUCE CAKE

This cake is light and delicious. It has a protein punch with the almond flour. It is egg free. I have created a streusel topping that is optional to make this more of a coffee cake. You will find that below the recipe, so remember to add it before baking if you want it. The cake is delicious either way.

¾ C brown rice flour
½ C almond flour
¼ C ground flax seed
1 tsp xantham gum
½ tsp ground allspice
½ tsp cinnamon
½ C firmly packed brown sugar
1 tsp baking soda
½ tsp salt
½ C water
½ C applesauce
¹⁄₃ C safflower oil (or coconut oil)
1 tsp Bragg's apple cider vinegar
½ C raisins (optional)

- Preheat oven to 350°. Measure all the almond flour, brown rice flour, brown sugar, baking soda, allspice, cinnamon, xanthan gum, salt, flax seed and mix together. Add the wet ingredients and stir until just combined. Add raisins if desired.
- Pour into an 8x8 baking dish and bake for 50 minutes.

Make a streusel topping for a coffee cake effect.

¼ C almonds chopped
¼ C walnuts chopped
¼ C brown sugar
2 T Earth Balance coconut butter

APPLE FRITTERS

Pure fall pleasure is found in these delectable apple fritters. They are easy to create and full of rich flavor. Use your favorite apples. Sour granny apples will stay very crunchy and create a nice tart contrast. Or use a soft red or yellow delicious for a soggy sweetness in the fritter. Either way, you will love them.

¾ C sweet rice flour (white rice)

¼ C arrowroot starch

¼ tsp xanthan gum

$^1/_3$ C organic cane sugar

¾ tsp salt

1 ½ tsp baking powder

1 tsp cinnamon

$^1/_3$ C almond milk mixed with
    ½ tsp lemon juice

1 egg, lightly beaten

1 C chopped gala apple, peeled

1-2 C high heat oil (like safflower oil)

- Combine flour, starch, xanthan gum, sugar, salt, baking powder and cinnamon in mixing bowl. Stir together milk and lemon juice until milk curdles. Lightly beat egg and combine with milk and stir into dry ingredients until just moist and mixed. Fold in chopped apple.
- Heat a medium cast iron skillet with about 1 C oil for frying. I use high heat safflower oil. Oil is ready when a little dough thrown in floats to top. Add the dough in heaping 1 T size.
- Cook until they are golden brown, about 2 minutes on each side. Place on paper towels as you remove them. Dust with powdered sugar. Or go crazy and glaze* them.

*Glaze

- In a small saucepan, heat 2 C of powdered sugar and 1½ T of almond milk. Heat and stir constantly until combined. Coat fritters in glaze and wait 3 minutes for it to harden.
- YUM!

earth jems

121

A CHOCOLATE HUG

These are a special treat for your GF chocolate lover! Chocolate ganache and raspberry filling make these cupcakes quite decadent and meet that chocolate craving!

¼ C coconut flour
¼ C cocoa powder
½ tsp baking soda
4 eggs
¼ C grape-seed oil
½ C honey
¼ tsp salt
6 T raspberry jam
fresh raspberries for decoration

- Preheat oven to 350°. Beat the eggs, oil, and honey on medium speed until well combined. Mix the dry ingredients, and add to the wet ingredients. Fill 12 cupcake liners ¼ full with the batter. Bake for 20 minutes. Use the clean toothpick test for done-ness. Let the cupcakes cool for 1 hour. Meanwhile, make the chocolate ganache.

Chocolate Ganache

This is a dairy-free ganache. It is rich and delicious!

8 oz Enjoy Life mini chocolate chips
1 tsp vanilla
1 can of coconut milk (not lite)

- Open the can of coconut milk and mix well in a mixing bowl with a whisk. Measure out ¾ of the coconut milk and pour it into a small sauce pan. Bring the milk to a boil on medium high, stirring constantly. As soon as it breaks a boil, remove from heat. Add chocolate chips and stir until melted. Add the vanilla. Set the mixture in the refrigerator until cooled and thickened. About 20 minutes.
- Once the cupcakes are cool, use a spoon to scoop out a hole in the top of the cupcake and put in 1 tsp of raspberry jam. Refill with cupcake. Stir the cooled ganache to loosen. Cover the cupcake with ganache, top with fresh raspberries and serve!

About the Author

Keena is a wife, mother of 3 girls, and a "continuing learner!" She studied Biology and graduated Summa Cum Laude with a B.S. in Biology from Moravian College in Pennsylvania. Keena worked in Aquaculture as a research scientist until her husband's career moved the family to Colorado. Keena says about her decision to stay home, "I decided that I wanted to be home with my kids and that has led us to a lot of life adventures. Schooling together gives us great family time to enjoy the outdoor activities that Colorado has to offer. I have always enjoyed learning and I wanted to give my children the same love and passion for learning."

Keena considers her blog and recipe "experimentation" a part of the research she loves to do. "I am enjoying searching for information and learning how to transfer that info into an easy way to understand. I am also enjoying my 'test kitchen' as I work to create healthy snacks that fit our nutritional needs and allergy restrictions. I strongly believe that God has put everything on Earth that we need to thrive as human beings. I don't believe we need to change those things very much to attain good nutrition." With all that said, enjoy Keena's first cookbook. And she wants your feedback, so please explore our website (www.earthjems.com) and feel free to comment, like, share and pass along to others as we grow together in this journey called life.

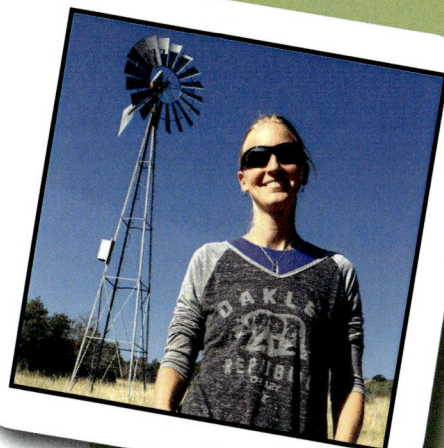

> **IT'S NOT HARD TO CHANGE YOUR LIFESTYLE. JUST REMEMBER – YOU'RE WORTH IT!**
> **–KEENA**

earthjems

INDEX

www.earthJEMS.com

INDEX

earth jems

D

www.earthJEMS.com

INDEX

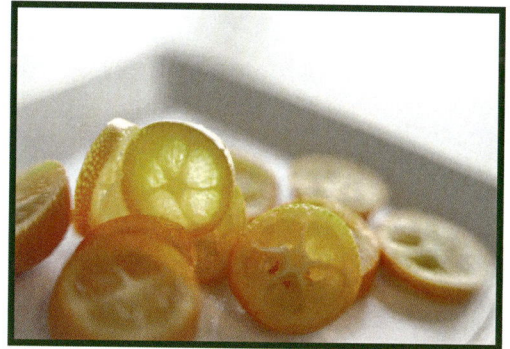

INDEX

H

I, J, K, L

M

INDEX

INDEX

N,O,P,Q,R,S

INDEX

earth jems

INDEX

🌿 Key

G **Gluten-free**

D **Dairy-free**

P **Paleo Friendly**

V **Vegan Friendly**

↻ **Restorative Diet* Friendly**

Recipe Measurements Key

[#]° = degrees Fahrenheit (USA)
[#]x[#] = pan measurements in inches
C= Cup
T = Tablespoon
tsp = teaspoon
GF = gluten-free

↻ * The restorative diet (look for Keena's Restorative Diet Cookbook coming soon!) is a method of eating to help decrease inflammation in your gut. This restorative diet allows cells to heal over a 7-10 day period so that the body won't react so much from food sensitivities and allows for healing. You will feel better, allowing your body to absorb more nutrients from your food. All the food in the restorative diet is grain-free with no sugars, limited in the ingredients and fairly simple on purpose to let your body start over so food sensitivities can be more easily recognized and foods may be re-introduced over time.

"CELEBRATE GOOD TIMES TOGETHER WITH FAMILY AND FRIENDS BY COOKING AND EATING TOGETHER FOR A HEALTHY LIFE."

-KEENA

MAIN DISHES

> "
> BEING HEALTHY ALSO MEANS FINDING A PLACE TO RELAX WHEREVER YOU ARE!
>
> –KEENA

Dinner is usually the big meal of the day where you get together with friends and family.

Asparagus Bowl